KiDS' COMPASS AMSTERDAM

CHEEKY MONKEYS

October 2014
ISBN 978-90-819852-2-2
Kids' Compass Amsterdam is published by Uitgeverij Cheeky Monkeys
www.kidscompassamsterdam.com

Authors: Janneke van Amsterdam and Dagmar Jeurissen
Art direction: Dagmar Jeurissen

Photohraphy by:
When not otherwise indicated all the photographs were provided by Amsterdam Marketing.
Photography on pages 25, 47, the cover and icons are by iStockphoto.com.

CONTENTS

Introduction	5
For parents - Practical information	6
Kids' info - Mokum here I come!	24
History - It all started with a swamp	38
Here we go! - Tourist information	46
The centre	48
Around the IJ lake and North Amsterdam	74
East Amsterdam	100
South Amsterdam	118
West Amsterdam	138
Active & sportive	146
Index	156

SYMBOLS

Monument, museum & fun

Park

Eating & drinking

Shopping

BABBOE City
www.babboe.com

INTRODUCTION

Ten years ago we wrote our first children's travel guide: Kidskompas Parijs. We 'borrowed' children from close friends and let them read our texts, and a few of them went with us on a city trip. Together we checked out the 'childproofness' of the Eiffel Tower, the Louvre museum and the Zoo de Vincennes. The children's travel guide about Paris became an instant success and was soon followed by guides about Barcelona and London.

Meanwhile we have children of our own and our boys - five in total - form a willing test team. For this travel guide - the first one in the English language - we stayed close to home. We both lived for many years in Amsterdam and are still very fond of this beautiful city. We want to share our enthousiasm with as many people as possible, preferably with other parents, as there are numerous fun things do to with children.

We want to make an excuse in advance for our English. As we write and publish the guide ourselves, we have to work with a very tight budget. For that reason we have decided to translate the texts ourselves. It is therefore inevitable that some mistakes have been made during translation and for this we want to offer you our sincere apologies.

Nevertheless we hope you will enjoy your stay in Amsterdam and we want to wish you a nice trip. Or as the Dutch say: goede reis!

Dagmar Jeurissen & Janneke van Amsterdam
tips@kidscompassamsterdam.com

FOR PARENTS

PRACTICAL INFORMATION

INFORMATION FOR PARENTS

You are going to Amsterdam. Maybe just for a day, but most probably you are spending the night. In this chapter we want to give parents useful information regarding hotels, public transportation and other practical issues. The other chapters in this book are written with children in mind so that they can explore the city with their own travel guide.

WHEN TO GO?

Visiting Amsterdam with children is fun in all seasons. Most museums and other attractions have expanded their children's programmes in recent years and much information aimed at children is also available in the English language. In this way all members of your travelling group will have a great and interesting time. The advantage of visiting the city in summer is that you can enjoy all kinds of activities on the water, but in winter there are many indoor activities. And who doesn't like ice skating on the Museumplein with the Rijksmuseum in the background? During Dutch school holidays it may be a bit busier in the city than usual but the advantage is that the number of children's activities also increases. For a list of Dutch school holidays see Schoolholidayseurope.com.

ONLINE PREPARATION

Obviously you can find all kinds of practical information regarding Amsterdam through the Internet, but use the Internet also for anticipatory pleasure. Visit the city with your children by using Google Earth for instance, or explore the websites of museums that you would like to visit during your stay and let the children figure out a convenient route through the city. Good to know: sometimes buying entrance tickets online means you get a discount, and - in some cases - you don't have to stand in line at the entrance. We recommend these fun sites and applications:

Practical websites and apps

iamsterdam.com The official online gateway to Amsterdam, with everything you want to know about the city, its attractions, events, hotels, restaurants, and much more. There is also a (free) I Amsterdam City Guide app

PLAY! Amsterdam Interactive application for finding one or more of the 427 playgrounds in Amsterdam. PLAY! Amsterdam costs 0.99 euro and is only available for Android.

TopTravelMaps App for iPad and iPhone with a map of the city that can also be used offline. Mark the location of your hotel, your car or favourite ice cream shop and you will find it again easily. The app is also available for Android and costs 0.99 euro.

Anne's Amsterdam With this free app you will see Amsterdam through the eyes of Anne Frank. Experience what life was like during the occupation in WWII. The app guides you to 30 historical sites in the city. Available for iPhone and Android.

9292-app Discover the fastest route by public transportation (including rail). Available for iPhone and Android, free.

Schiphol Airport app With this app you can check departure and arrival times, reserve a taxi or use the airport map to find your way around. Available for iPhone and Android, free.

Tales & Tours Use your phone as a personal guide. This app offers free and paid digital guides & tours around the city. Find guides for cycling, walking and more. Available for iPhone and Android, free.

Babbel Learn Dutch! The Babbel application has a wide variety of courses. We wish you good luck or as we say in Duch: veel succes!

Getting there

Arriving in Amsterdam by car means you will have to take the **A10 motorway**. This motorway is the ring road around the city of Amsterdam ('Ring Amsterdam'). The A10 has eighteen exits, also called **S-routes**. Each S-route takes you to a different part of town. It is therefore useful to know which S-route you have to take to get to your final destination. Each S-route is indicated with an 'S' followed by a three digit number starting at 100. Depending on your final destination it might be practical to use one of the large **P+R car parks** (Park & Ride) on the outskirts of the city and continue your journey by public transport. After all, the city centre is very busy and has a lot of one-way streets that are very narrow. In addition to that, driving (and parking) along canals can be quite an adventure. Parking outside the city centre also saves a lot of money because the parking fee downtown is 5 euros per hour. The P+R car parks are already signposted on the A10.
When parking at one of the P+R car parks outside the city, you can use public transport to get into the city. You can park your car for example at the **Transferium of the Amsterdam Arena**. You pay 2.20 euros per hour with a maximum of 22 euros for 24

hours. The P+R at the **World Fashion Centre** (exit S106 on the A10) is even cheaper. At this car park the parking fee is 8 euros for 24 hours, including free public transport. The same rate applies to the P+R car parks in **Zeeburg** (S114), **Gaasperplas** (exit S113), **Sloterdijk** (S102), and **Bos en Lommer** (exit S104 or S105). Since 2013 it is no longer required to put a parking ticket behind your windscreen. The digital parking system in Amsterdam means that you need to enter your registration plate details into the parking meter when you pay for parking. Amsterdam's parking meters do not accept cash or coins. Payments can only be made using a Dutch bank card or any major (international) credit card. *For more information visit Iamsterdam.com*

Arriving by train or plane

Amsterdam has several train stations but if you arrive in Amsterdam by train it is most likely that your journey ends at **Amsterdam Central Station**. From there you can use all kinds of public transport to get to your hotel or appartment.

Amsterdam Airport Schiphol, the primary international airport in the Netherlands, is located about 20 kilometres from Amsterdam. You can reach the city from Schiphol in just half an hour by **train** or **taxi**.

At the exit you will find the taxi stand from Schiphol Airport. A ride to the city centre costs about 40 euros and takes about half an hour. Via Schiphol.nl you can also book a taxi to and from Amsterdam. You can opt for a private taxi, or a shared one. When you booked a taxi in advance go to the Schiphol Transfer Assistance at Schiphol Plaza (Arrivals 4, open 24/7). *Also check Schiphol.nl for up to date information*

SCHIPHOL IS ONE OF THE MAJOR AIRPORTS IN EUROPE AND IN 2013 IT WAS USED BY 56.2 MILLION PASSENGERS. ARE YOU AND YOUR CHILDREN WONDERING HOW SUCH A BIG AIRPORT OPERATES? PARTICIPATE IN THE SCHIPHOL BEHIND THE SCENES TOUR AND DISCOVER SPOTS YOU WOULD OTHERWISE NEVER SEE, THE LARGE HANGARS FOR EXAMPLE, AND THE SNOW FLEET. THE TOUR TAKES ABOUT AN HOUR. VISIT SCHIPHOLBEHINDTHESCENES.NL FOR MORE INFORMATION.

Public transport chip card

Since 2014, everyone traveling by public transport in the Netherlands is required to have a public transport chip card (**'OV-chipkaart'**). Residents in Amsterdam own a personalised card, but it is also possible to purchase a non-personalised card that can be (re)charged. The chip card costs around 7.50 euros. You can also opt for the **GVB day passes** for unlimited travel, available for 1 to 7 days. These passes are valid on trams, buses and metros operated by GVB Amsterdam.

When using any form of public transport you will have to **check in and check out**. This is done by holding the card up to the card reader until you see a green light and you hear a beep. On trams and buses the readers are situated at the doors. If travelling by train or metro you can find free-standing poles near the entrance or exit. You will have to check in when you enter the tram, metro, train or bus and when you leave the vehicule you will have to check out.

The non-personalised chip card is available at some 4,000 stores in the Netherlands (including supermarkt chain Albert Heijn). On the website Ov-chipkaart.nl you can easily find the nearest point of sale. GVB day passes can be bought with the driver or conductor, at sales machines in metro stations, at VVV offices and at GWK offices.

Reduced price for children

Children under 3 years travel for free. Children 4 through 11 years that are under supervision of at least one adult travel at a heavily reduced price. For 2.50 euros you can buy a **day ticket for children** that is valid for 24 hours.

Tourist office VVV

The headquarters of the Amsterdam Tourist Office (VVV) are located directly opposite **Central Station** in the Noord-Zuid Hollands Koffiehuis (the white building at the waterfront). You can also find a tourist agency on the **Leidseplein** (Ticketshop Leidseplein). You can contact the tourist office for information, excursions and tours, maps, guides, hotel reservations and tickets for public transport.

I amsterdam City Card

The I amsterdam City card can be bought for 24 (47 euro), 48 (57 euro) or 72 (67 euro) hours and it will give you **free admission** to a whole list of attractions including a free canal cruise. You also get a detailed city map, and you can make free use of all tram, bus and metro lines of the Municipal Transport Company Amsterdam (GVB). The card is certainly a good deal if you are planning to visit a lot of attractions. For example NEMO (science museum) and Artis (the zoo) are free of admission and this will save almost 35 euros per person. For children up to 10 years it's often better not to buy the card since they allready get a discount at most museums. On the website Iamsterdam.com you can find a detailed list of entrance prices of most attractions in Amsterdam (without the I amsterdam City Card), so you can easily calculate if the card is a good bargain. The I amsterdam City Card can be bought online, but you have to pick it up at one of the two Visitor Information Centres. There is also a City Card app. *More information + online buying: www.iamsterdam.com*

Getting around

With skates, by bike, by boat, on a board or just on foot: there are plenty of opportunities to get around in Amsterdam. A number of options will be discussed in another chapter. Moving around by bicycle for example (see page 151) or on water (see page 148). But consider also the following possibilities:

Tram and metro

Amsterdam has an extensive **tram network** and almost all trams depart from Central Station. At the stops there are route maps showing you what tram number you need to take to get to your destination. Remember that the lines 1, 2 and 5 pass Dam square and the Leidsestraat to arrive at the Leidseplein. Lines 4, 9, 16 and 24 ride along the Rokin to the Munt. Most trams have a conductor, so you have to get in in the front or at the back. There are **four metro lines** in Amsterdam. The lines 51, 53 and 54 leave from Central Station. Currently a fifth metro line is being constructed: the North/South line which will be operational in 2017.

Taxis

The taxi is a popular means of transport in Amsterdam but since the traffic is dense at some hours, sometimes patience is a virtue. From 2013 only so-called TTO's have to right to

I amsterdam®
city card

4
Station RA
2136

carry passengers. This Approved Taxi Organisation is approved by the municipality. You can find official taxi ranks at various locations in the city and they are indicated by blue signs. But what can you expect from such an official taxi ride? The taxi driver takes the shortest route to your place of destination, he has a visible meter and at the end of the trip you will get a receipt. The fee you will have to pay depends on the number of kilometres (2.08 euro per km), the duration of the ride (0.34 cents per minute) and you also pay a boarding fee of 2.83 euros.

Green taxi

Grab a 'green' taxi, for example an **electric Tuk Tuk**. These vehicles are environmentally friendly and they can take up to six people, so they are also suitable for families. At Central Station you'll find a boarding point for green taxis. *See also www.tuktuksightseeing.eu*
Since several years **pedicabs** cruise the streets of Amsterdam. They are a nice alternative to regular taxis. Of course you can use a pedicab to take you from location A to location B, but you can also make a tour through the city. 1.5-2 hours is enough to see a large part of Amsterdam. The driver/guide is Dutch, but normally also fluent in English. A 1.5 hour tour costs around 40-60 euros and a pedicab is suitable for two adults and two small children. Reservations can be made through the website, but you can also just hail one on the street, especially around Dam square and Central Station. *More information Amsterdam-fietstaxi.nl*

IT MAY SOUND CORNY BUT LIKE IN ANY OTHER BIG CITY IT IS GOOD TO PAY EXTRA ATTENTION TO THE TRAFFIC. ESPECIALLY IN AMSTERDAM IT CAN BE QUITE CONFUSING WITH ALL THE BIKES, TRAMS AND TAXIS. AMSTERDAM IS ALSO NOTORIOUS FOR PICK-POCKETS.

Coach

You can also opt for a city tour by coach. Coaches depart from Dam square and you make a tour of 20, 30 or 45 minutes through the old city centre. The coach driver is also your guide and he will give you lots of information about the city. It is not necessary to make a reservation, just go to Dam square each day between 11 am and 6 pm. Good to know: coaches are suitable for groups up to four people and in bad weather and in winter coaches ride according to a different time table. *More information karos.nl*

Public holidays

At public holidays shops, museums and attractions usually close earlier or are closed all day. These are the Dutch public holidays in 2015: January 1 (New Year), April 5 (Easter Sunday), April 6 (Easter Monday), April 27 (King's Day), May 5 (Liberation Day), May 14 (Ascension Day), May 24 (Pentecost Sunday), May 25 (Pentecost Monday), December 25 (Christmas Day), December 26 (Boxing Day).

Opening hours

Shops are generally open from 9 am to 6 pm, except Saturdays until 5 pm, Thursdays until 9 pm and Sundays from noon to 5 pm. Most supermarkets close at 8 pm or 10 pm.

Emergencies

As in all big cities, be aware of pickpockets, especially when travelling by public transport. In case of an emergency call 112. When you need medical assistance you can call the tourist doctor on + 31 (0)20 4275011.

Places to stay

Amsterdam has over 400 hotels, but there are also some nice alternatives. In the following pages we would like to give you some insider information regarding nice places to stay. Also search online and read reviews from other families who already have visited the Dutch capital.

Camping

Amsterdam has six campsites, including the new Amsterdam City Camp in the North of Amsterdam (across the IJ), intended for campers. Other campsites are Camping Badhoeve (at the Kinselmeer lake), Camping Vliegenbos, Camping Zeeburg (10-15 minutes from the city centre. At this site you can rent nicely coloured wagonettes), Camping Gaasper Amsterdam (15 minutes from the city centre), Camping Hostel Amsterdam (in the Amsterdamse Bos. *More information: Amsterdamcitycamp.nl, Campingdebadhoeve.nl, Vliegenbos.com, Campingzeeburg.nl, Gaaspercamping.nl, Campingamsterdam.nl.*

Camping Vliegenbos

Are you looking for an original stay surrounded by greenery, yet close to the city? Then Camping Vliegenbos is the right place to go. At this camp site in the north of Amsterdam you can stay in your tent, camper or caravan, but it is much more fun to stay in the **Camping Hotel** or in one of the **cabins**. The cabins are actually 'art cabins', decorated by young Amsterdam designers. The hotel consists of twenty tents situated around an outdoor kitchen and hangout spot. You sleep in your own tent, but because of the shared facilities you easily connect with other campers. There are also a restaurant with terrace and a camping shop on site. The ferry arriving at the rear of Amsterdam Central Station is a 15 minutes walk away which means that it will take you only 20 minutes to get in the city centre. City buses 32 and 33 stop at 200 meters from the campsite. Read more about the Vliegenbos on page 97. *More information www.vliegenbos.com*

Airbnb

On Airbnb.nl you can find a wide variety of places to stay, from an apartment in the Pijp to a houseboat or family house in the Jordaan. The prices are often quite reasonable and staying in a private house has many advantages. You can cook if you want to and often the atmosphere in the house is more cosy than in a hotel. You can also read reviews from previous visitors and if you are lucky there are toys for the children.

Bed & breakfast

You have also plenty of options when you would like to stay in a bed and breakfast. For example, look at Bedandbreakfast.nl and read the feedback from previous guests. BBwelcome2amsterdam.nl has four small houses in the north of Amsterdam for rent. Two of them are suitable for four people. The locations can be reached by using the (free) ferry at the rear of Central Station. Another tip: B&B Lieve Nachten ('Sweet Nights' in English) on Amsterdam IJburg. This is one of the most child-friendly neighbourhoods in Amsterdam, with plenty of entertainment (swimming!) around the corner, beautiful rooms and a lovely garden. *More information Lievenachten.nl*

Hostel

There are several hostels in Amsterdam where you can stay at a decent price. People travelling with children often have to book a private room. Especially the Stayokay hostel at the Vondelpark (see picture below) is terrific. There are rooms for 4-6 persons (with private shower and toilet). The longer in advance you can book, the greater the chance that there are still rooms available. There are also Stayokay hostels in Zeeburg (actually a design hotel) and at Stadsdoelen, just a stone's throw away from Dam square. *See Stayokay.com*

Stayokay Vondelpark

MAGAZINE

A-Mag is the English city magazine about Amsterdam. There are six issues a year and it offers tips regarding eating, shopping, excursions, (family) activities, things going on in the city and more. On the website Iamsterdam.com you can browse through the digital version of the most current issue. You can also buy A-Mag for 2.95 euros at several bookstores in the city, and in some hotels you get the magazine for free.

ACTIVITIES AND EVENTS

Throughout the year numerous activities, events and festivals are organized in Amsterdam. On Iamsterdam.com you can find a comprehensive and detailed overview, we already give a few tips for people travelling with children. Note that most museums and attractions organize special children's activities during school holidays. When staying in Amsterdam during one of those holidays, check the websites of the museums you plan on visiting for the most up to date information. Not all events may be equally suitable for foreign visitors, and not all activities listed have a website in English.

JANUARY

Amsterdam Light Festival

During the Amsterdam Light Festival light will play a central role in the city as museums and institutions organize light-related activities, introducing visitors to innovations in light art.
Amsterdamlightfestival.com

National Tulip Day

During the National Tulip Day ('Nationale Tulpendag') everyone can pick tulips for free on Dam square. This day is the official start of the tulip season.
Check Iamsterdam.com for the exact date

FEBRUARY

Chinese New Year

In February the Chinese New Year is celebrated in China Town. Go to the Nieuwmarkt and the immediate vicinity for all kinds of festivities including a colourful dragon parade. Nice to know: 2015 is the year of the goat, 2016 the year of the monkey.
The exact date changes ecery year, 2015: 19 February, 2016: 8 February and 2017: 28 January

APRIL

Imagine Film Festival

This yearly international film festival takes place in the EYE Filmmuseum. For children, there is a special programme. *Imaginefilmfestival.nl*

King's Day

Since 2014 the people in the Netherlands celebrate King's Day ('Koningsdag') in stead of Queen's Day. On this day the whole country celebrates king Willem-Alexander. The city turns orange and throughout Amsterdam musical performances are organized. With children go to the children's flea market in the Vondelpark.

27 april, door de hele stad, info via Iamsterdam.com en Bredewegfestival.nl

Egg hunt in Artis

In Artis (the zoo) children can partake in all kids of activities on Easter Sunday, including a treasure egg hunt.

www.artis.nl.

MAY

Food Film Festival

This festival is a three-day international event regarding food. With documentaries, films, workshops, lectures and a special children's programme with 'blind' tasting and culinary performances. The festival always takes place in spring at the Westergasfabriek.

Foodfilmfestival.nl

Puppet show at Dam square

From May to mid October every Sunday a puppet show is organised at Dam square. There are performances at 1, 2, 3 and 4 pm. If it is raining the puppet show moves to the Beurs

van Berlage, right across Dam square.
Poppenkastopdedam.nl

Hemeltjelief Festival

The Hemeltjelief Festival (around Ascension Day) is suitable for the whole family. With art, theater, music and a children's festival. Location: the NDSM yard in the north of Amsterdam.
Hemeltjelieffestival.nl

Open Air Theatre Vondelpark

All summer you can visit numerous performances, including special performances for children, in the open air theatre in the Vondelpark.
From May, Openluchttheater.nl

Rolling kitchens

On the grounds of the former gasworks dozens of rolling kitchens gather, making it a great outdoor restaurant. You can find all kinds of chefs, from an eccentric foodtruck to a rhubarb pizza chef. For children there are a carousel and ferris wheel, and what about homemade candy, chocolate fondue and delicious ice cream?
Rollendekeukens.nl

JUNE/JULY

ZOOmer evenings

Every Saturday in June, July and August the zoo Artis is open until sunset. Enjoy a picnic and the extra activities that are being organized.
Artis.nl

WESTwaARTs

The organizers call it the best summer festival in the west of Amsterdam: WESTwaARTs ('Westward'). The nice thing about this festival is that it lasts for more than a month. In June and July cultural Sunday sessions take place with music, theatre, workshops, tasty foods and drinks and much more. The festival takes place in the Erasmus Park and Art for Kids presents all kids of theatre for children. There is also a special terrace for children's workshops.
Podiummozaiek.nl/programmaPodiummozaiek.nl/programma

Kwaku Summer Festival

This festival started once as a soccer tournament for children who could not go on vacation. Meanwhile, it is one of the biggest festivals in Amsterdam. During five weekends there are all kinds of celebrations in the Bijlmerpark with music, food, drink, dance, debates, lectures and of course there is still football. For kids aged 5-14 years there are children's work-

shops with painting, music, rap and dance.
Kwakufestival.nl

Over het IJ Festival

The Over het IJ Festival takes place in the north of Amsterdam at the former NDSM shipyard. Take the ferry behind Central Station and within a few minutes you are surrounded by bustling theatre performances. There is theatre, several live bands, great food and performances in sea containers. Artists of the NDSM Children's Workplace help children to build their own city and often there is a special family show. The performances in the shipping containers are also fun for kids.
Overhetij.nl

AUGUST

Junior Canal Festival

This is the children's version of the famous Canal Festival ('Grachtenfestival'), which is dedicated to classical music. Throughout the city performances and workshops are being organized. Fun: check out the special baby concerts.
Juniorgrachtenfestival.nl

Parade

The traveling theatre festival the Parade has set up its tents again in the Martin Luther King Park in the south of Amsterdam. Each afternoon children can visit the Children's Parade.
Deparade.nl

Junior Canal Festival

Uitmarkt

The Uitmarkt is a three-day celebration of the Dutch cultural scene. It is the largest annual festival in the country, officially launching the new cultural season by showcasing the very best in music, art, theatre, dance, opera, literature and cabaret performances. Performances are held outdoors and indoors at numerous theatres, museums and venues near the Leidseplein and the Museumplein.
Uitmarkt.nl

SEPTEMBER

Open Monumentendag

At Open Monumentendag (Heritage Day) sixty monuments open their doors for the general public. For addresses check the website.
Second weekend in September, Openmonumentendag.nl

OCTOBER

Cinekid

International Film, Television and Media Festival for Youth, with of course a lot of movies, but also seminars and workshops. Check the program on the website.
Cinekid.nl

NOVEMBER

Gnome hunt

Look for forest gnomes in the Amsterdamse Bos (forest of Amsterdam). For children from 3 to 6 years; the tour starts at the Visitor Centre.
Amsterdamsebos.nl

Museum Night

Fifty Amsterdam museums open their doors until 2 am with special programs. Look for participating museums on the website
Information and tickets Museumnachtamsterdam.nl

The arrival of Sinterklaas

The arrival of Sinterklaas (the Dutch equivalent of Santa Claus) consists of a long parade that goes through the city. Look at the website for the exact route. Also nice: a visit to department store the Bijenkorf near Dam square. Here you can see two giant Black Peters (the assistants of Sinterklaas) climbing up on ropes. Sinterklaas always arrives around the 17th of November.
Sintinamsterdam.nl

A child dressed up as the assistant of Sinterklaas

KIDS' INFO

MOKUM HERE I COME!

Mokum here I come!

You are going to Amsterdam or maybe you are already there. With the Kids Compass travel guide you will discover all the exciting things that can be done in the city, and we also give you lots of fun facts about the Dutch, Amsterdam and its residents. For example, what are typical Amsterdam dishes you definitely have to taste? What about all the water in the city? And did you know that Amsterdam is also called Mokum? Have fun!

The Dutch capital

Amsterdam is the official capital of the Netherlands, but the government resides in The Hague. This is quite strange because in most countries the prime minsters and his colleagues reside in the capital. The king and queen of the Netherlands use Amsterdam and not The Hague for celebratory purposes. A big event was the coronation of king Willem-Alexander in 2013.

MOKUM IS ANOTHER NAME FOR AMSTERDAM. THE WORD COMES FROM HEBREW AND MEANS 'PLACE' OR 'CITY'. THE WORD WAS FORMERLY USED BY JEWISH PEOPLE LIVING IN THE CITY.

Fun facts

Amsterdam has...

* 165 **canals** (this is why Amsterdam is sometimes called the Venice of the north)
* 1,539 **bridges**
* 2,500 **house boats**
* inhabitants from **175 different countries**
* more than 400,000 **trees**
* more than 30 **parks and big gardens**
* 51 **museums**
* a special boot for **stray cats**
* the most **narrow** house of Europe
* the **Amsterdam Arena**, the first football stadium in Europe with a sliding roof

On the website Iamsterdam.com you can find more fun facts and figures.

The Netherlands

* The country is divided into 12 **provinces**.
* Since 2013 the Netherlands have a new king: **king Willem-Alexander.**
* The king is married to **Maxima** from Argentina and they have three daugters.
* In the Netherlands there are twice as many **bicycles** as there are cars.
* **Windmills, tulips, wooden shoes and cheese** are considered as real Dutch icons. But do you actually see people walking on wooden shoes?
* Dutch children start **school** at the age of 4 and they have to bring their own lunch.
* **School times** are from 8.30 am tot 3 pm.
* Dutch school children don't wear a **school uniform**.

Numerous canals

Amsterdam has more than one hundred kilometers of canals. The four main canals are **the Singel, the Herengracht, the Keizersgracht and the Prinsengracht.** They are dug in de 17th century – in a period called the Golden Age. Alongside the canals are lots of monumental buildings. In the old days these were the houses of the rich and nowadays it is still very expensive to buy such a house. Maybe this comes as a surprise, but many of the houses have large, green gardens at the back. Since 2010, the Amsterdam canals are on the World Heritage List meaning that they are considered to be a masterpiece.

Magere Brug / Skinny Bridge

Famous Bridges

If you are in the centre of Amsterdam you will see canals everywhere. When there are many canals there obviously also have to be many bridges to cross them. In total, there are nearly 1,300 bridges in Amsterdam, of which 80 are located within the area of the four main canals. Maybe now you understand why some people call Amsterdam the Venice of the North (because the city has so many canals and bridges). However, if you properly count them all you will notice that Amsterdam has even more bridges than Venice. So Venice is actually the Amsterdam of the South! There are a few very famous and special bridges in Amsterdam. The **Magere Brug** ('Skinny Bridge') for example often feautures in movies. Maybe you have seen it in the James Bond movie Diamonds are Forever. The oldest bridge in Amsterdam is the **Torensluis**, which was built in 1648. Once there was a prison in the Torensluis and you can still see its barred windows. This bridge is a 5-minute walk from Dam square, at the Singel.

Other famous bridges have won prizes, such as the long, red serpentine bridge between Sporenburg and Borneo Island in the east of Amsterdam. This bridge is 93 meters long and is also called the **Python Bridge** (a python is a snake). The **Nesciobrug** - between IJburg and the Watergraafsmeer - is the longest cycle and pedestrian bridge in the Netherlands.

Exploring Amsterdam

The city of Amsterdam can be explored in a lot of different fun ways:

The Floating Dutchman

When you enter the Floating Dutchman it looks like you are boarding a regular tourist bus. You discover the streets of Amsterdam but… all of a sudden the bus drives straight into a canal! That is what we call a fun and original way to discover the city. De bus leaves at Lovers Van Gogh Café opposite Central Station and plunges into the water at the NEMO science museum. After a tour of the canals you exit the water again at NEMO. The tour lasts about two hours and you will drive/sail for example to the Maritime Museum, the Hermitage museum and the Skinny Bridge. Tickets for this tour can be purchased through the website or at any of the outlets of Rederij Lovers. The tourist information on board of the Floating Dutchman is available in several languages. *Location: 25 Prins Hendrikkade, 020 5301090, floatingdutchman.nl. Departure: Tue-Sun 11 am, 2 and 5 pm. Admission € 22, 4-12 years € 17*

THIS BUS IS ALSO CALLED AN AMPHIBIOUS BUS, BECAUSE AMPHIBIANS ARE ANIMALS THAT CAN LIVE BOTH ON LAND AND IN WATER. FROGS AND TOADS FOR EXAMPLE. CAN YOU THINK OF MORE EXAMPLES?

Canal cruise

In Amsterdam it is fun to make a cruise throught the canals. On the Lovers and Canal Company websites you can get information in all kinds of cruises. How about a cruise through the port of Amsterdam, a pizza cruise, a trip along the hundred highlights of the city or a cruise by night? Both cruise companies also have a special hop on, hop off boat. *For information visit lovers.nl or canal.nl*

TIP! LOVERS HAS A ARTIS ROYAL ZOO EXPRESS (SEE PAGE 110). THIS CRUISE TAKES YOU FROM AMSTERDAM CENTRAL STATION TO THE ARTIS ZOO. ON THE WAY BACK YOU WILL GET A CANAL CRUISE.

Hop-on, hop-off bus

You can also explore Amsterdam in a bus with a panoramic roof. Buy a ticket at City Sightseeing Amsterdam, and get on the bus! The hop-on hop-off service offers you the chance to hop on and hop off at any of the centrally located stops and visit numerous attractions and museums. *More information: citysightseeingamsterdam.nl*

HOLLAND
GELDER
LAND
ZEELAND
I amsterdam

Canal bike

Do you want a little bit more action? Then go canal biking and discover spots you otherwise wouldn't see. Two people pedal, other passengers relax in the back and keep an eye on the water map. Lifevestst are available at the rental piers and children who want to pedal themselves must have a swimming certificate. A reservation is not required and when it is raining – and in The Netherlands that is often the case – they will pop a hood on your canal bike. There are three rental piers: at the Leidseplein, the Rijksmuseum, and the Anne Frank Museum). *For more information 020 2170500, canal.nl. Open: daily 10 am to 5 pm. Rental fee € 8 p.p. for 1 hour*

Bike rental

You can also explore Amsterdam like the Dutch do: by bike. It is a lot faster than walking and you will never have to wait at a tram or bus stop. For bike rental addresses see page 151. But we have to warn you for the traffic in Amsterdam. Especially in the city centre the streets are very crowded and narrow, and cycling across tram rails can be quite an adventure. So you must pay extra attention when riding your bike. Therefore some useful advice:

* Make sure your intentions are clear to everyone on the road. Ride in a straight line and signal turns with your arm. Check behind you before turning or changing lanes.
* Watch out for tram rails. When your tires get stuck in them, you will fall down. Cross them slowly and in a straight angle.
* Make sure you have a detailed map of all the city streets. When renting a bike you often get one for free.
* Always lock your bike, even when you think you can keep an eye on it.

LEARNING DUTCH

Although most people in The Netherlands speak very good English, it might be nice if you can talk some Dutch. Just try it!

English	Dutch	Pronunciation
no	nee	nay
yes	ja	jaw
my name is...	ik heet	ik hayt
I am from...	ik kom uit...	ik kom ijt
one	een	ayn
two	twee	tway
three	drie	dree
four	vier	veer
five	vijf	vife

English	Dutch	Pronunciation
six	zes	zes
seven	zeven	zayvun
eight	acht	awgt
nine	negen	naygun
ten	tien	teen
ice cream	ijsje	ysju
pancake	pannenkoek	pahnuncook
croquette	kroket	crocat
nice	lekker	lekur
good morning	goedemorgen	goodumorgun
goodbye	tot ziens	tot zeens
bye	doei	dooy
all well?	alles goed?	ahlus good?
The Netherlands	Nederland	naydurlahnd
Amsterdam	Amsterdam	Ahmsturdam

Famous Poles

Maybe you have noticed them already in the streets of Amsterdam: the red bollards on the pavement. They have three crosses, the Andreas Crosses, coming from the city arms. The first Amsterdammertjes were placed in the 18th century to make a distinction between the road and the sidewalk. This reduced the risk that a horse and carriage ran into a house. Especially after World War II, the poles were often used to prevent people from parking their cars wherever they liked.

Eating and Drinking

In Amsterdam you can eat dishes from all over the world. Restaurant Bazar Amsterdam, (see picture on the next page) located in a suburb called the Pijp, is worth a try. The restaurant is hidden behind the doors of an old church and when entering it feels like you step into an Oriental fairy tale. Enjoy the upbeat music, the colorful décor, the beautiful chandeliers and a menu with all kinds of delicious snacks from North Africa and the Middle East. There is a special children's menu, a video corner and there are plenty of games and toys available (Location: 182 Albert Cuypstraat, Bazaramsterdam.nl). But there are also some typical Dutch dishes to eat in Amsterdam. The following snacks are worth a try:

Kroket (croquette)

A kroket is a deep fried ragout filled snack coated with breadcrumbs. You can eat it separately or on a sandwich. Dutch people combine a kroket with some mustard. You can order a kroket in a bar but also in a snackbar. Try to find one with a wall of little glass doors (often called Febo). Just put a coin in the machine, open one of the little doors and grab your snack.

Patatje Oorlog

Dutch people like to combine their fries with peanut sauce, mayonnaise and onions. This dish is called a 'patatje oorlog' (literally translated: war fries).

Kapsalon

The latest snack trend: fries covered with shawarma (grilled and sliced meat), melted cheese and salad. The Dutch call this a 'kapsalon' (literally translated: hair salon).

Pannenkoek and poffertjes

Pannenkoeken (pancakes) are probably familiar but what about poffertjes? A poffertje is a small, fluffy pancake. They taste really nice with powdered sugar and some butter. You can order pancakes at most pancake restaurants and sometimes you can buy them in little food stalls in the street.

Oliebollen

Oliebollen (Dutch donuts) are fried dough balls (with or without raisins in it) and in winter they are sold in special food stalls. You eat them with powdered sugar.

Licorice

Black candy in different shapes and sizes with the taste of aniseed. You can buy it in every supermarket, just look for a box with 'drop' written on it. Every year Dutch people eat around two kilograms of drop per person.

Hagelslag

Chocolate sprinkles are called 'hagelslag' and the Dutch eat this on a sandwich.

Herring

Haring (herring) is a salted fish that is eaten raw with onions. The way the Dutch eat it is as

Restaurant Bazar Amsterdam

follows: just grap the tail, put your head backwards and let the fish slide into your mouth.

Amsterdammertje

An Amsterdammertje is a round cake filled with almond paste.

Stroopwafels

Stroopwafels (syrup waffles) are two flat waffles with caramel syrup in between. They are available in every super market and at most bakeries. Yammie.

Breakfast and dinner

For breakfast and lunch Dutch people eat slices of bread with cheese, meat or chocolate sprinkles. Diner is often served around six o'clock.

Mashed potatoes

In winter time the Dutch eat a lot of mashed potatoes, combined with different kind of cabbage. Think of sauerkraut, kale, endive and carrots with onions. The dish is usually combined with a smoked sausage, meatball or beef. In winter also try pea soup ('erwtensoep').

A baby is born!

When a baby is born, people in the Netherlands eat biscuit rusk with candy-covered aniseed. Blue for a boy, pink for a girl.

AMSTERDAM FACADES

Look around as you walk through the centre of Amsterdam. You will notice that no house is the same but still there are some similarities. Try to find the following facades:

Wooden facade: this is difficult since there remain only two wooden facades in Amsterdam, namely at 34 Begijnhof and 1 Zeedijk. This is not so strange considering the fact that wood burns very easily.

Stepped gable: this facade looks like a giant step. These gables where very popular in the 17th century.

Spout gable: a spout gable can be found at warehouses from the 17th century. These gables are quite ordinary and they have a rectangular construction at the top. You can find nice spout gables at the Brouwersgracht.

Neck gable: this type of gable is typical for narrow houses. It consists of a broad straight segment with rounded contours (the shoulders).

Bell gable: the top of this gable looks like a bell.

Cornice gable: this gable makes a pointed roof appear straight.

able

Stepped gable

gable

Spout gable

HISTORY

IT ALL STARTED WITH A SWAMP

The feast of St. Nicholas by Jan Steen

THE HISTORY OF AMSTERDAM

You probably think that the history of Amsterdam is a boring subject, but actually it is not so bad. If we had the time, we could write lots of books about it, with all kinds of fascinating stories. But don't worry: we didn't do it. In the next pages we will only introduce you to some important people and events.

AT THE VERY BEGINNING

The very beginning of Amsterdam dates back to the year 1000, when the area was still a large wetland. Around that time it was called **Aemestelle**. A wetland is a kind of swamp, meaning that the surface is not actually land, but also not actually water. It was mostly very muddy. But people wanted to live in Aemestelle and they wanted to grow food, so the water had to disappear. The people started digging ditches and it worked! But to keep the country really dry, it was important that **dikes** were being constructed.

THE DAM

In the 13th century, dikes were constructed along the Zuiderzee (currently the IJsselmeer), the IJ (this was a bay of the Zuiderzee) and the Amstel river. Little by little the land was impoldered and in the 13th century a fishing village arose at the mouth of the Amstel river. In 1204 a local rich man built a castle here and about 60 years later a dam was constructed on the Amstel (from that moment the village was called Amsteldam). On the dike along the west bank of the Amstel (nowadays the Nieuwendijk) the first houses were built. Around the year 1225, the first (wooden) houses were also built on the dike on the east side (currently the Warmoestraat).

IN 1421 AND 1452 THERE WAS A GREAT FIRE IN THE CITY AND ALMOST ALL THE WOODEN HOUSES WENT UP IN FLAMES. YOU CAN FIND THE OLDEST REMAINING HOUSE AT 34 BEGIJNHOF. THIS IS NEAR THE BIG SHOPPING STREET KALVERSTRAAT. THE HOUSE WAS BUILT IN 1425 AND IS CALLED HET HOUTEN HUYS (MEANING THE HOUSE OF WOOD).

Beer and wool

Around 1300 Amsterdam received city rights and trade with other countries was becoming increasingly important. There was a lot of beer import from Hamburg, later followed by wool, wood and corn. Much of the trade took place around the **Warmoesstraat** and at the end of the Middle Ages this was the wealthiest street in Amsterdam. Between 1300 and the first half of the 15th century the city was growing so fast that it had to be **extended** three times with new canals and bridges.

The Golden Age

In the 16th century Amsterdam became the largest port in the world. Banks established themselves in the city and because everyone had the right to believe in whatever he wished (Amsterdam had **religious freedom**), scholars from around the world started living here. As a result the city got bigger and bigger, and during the 17th century the famous **canals** were constructed, which is where rich merchants built their warehouses. Craftsmen on the other hand moved to the **Jordaan** where they built workplaces and houses.
In the Golden Age, the **Dutch East India Company** was founded. This **trade organization** sent ships to China and Indonesia to bring plenty of spices, wood and other merchandise to the Netherlands. In the Maritime Museum (Scheepvaartmuseum, see page 79) you can admire one of their ships: the Amsterdam.

TO WORK ON A SHIP YOU HAD TO BE 13 YEARS OLD. A SAILOR EARNED ABOUT 110 GUILDERS A YEAR. THAT'S CURRENTLY ABOUT 50 EUROS. FUN FACT: IN 1682 THERE WERE SIX MONKEYS, TWELVE PARROTS, TWO COCKATOOS, A CROCODILE AND A MOOSE TRANSPORTED ON A TRADE SHIP. COOL!.

Famous painters

At the beginning of the 17th century there were a lot of painters living in Amsterdam. Many people were rich, so there was enough money to buy art. Famous painters living in the 17th century were **Rembrandt van Rijn, Jan Steen and Johannes Vermeer**. Rembrandt van Rijn is one of the most famous Dutch painters of the Golden Age. But he was more than a painter. He made around 300 paintings, but also 2000 drawings and 300 etchings. Etching involves sheets of metal, usually made of copper or zinc, and acid used to etch the print onto the metal. The most famous painting of Rembrandt is **The Night Watch** and this painting can be seen in the Rijksmuseum. Rembrandt was a very funny man. He spent all

the money he earned on art and fancy clothing and one day he even went bankrupt. Rembrandt eventually died in 1669 in Amsterdam and was buried in the Westerkerk.

FUN: BUILD YOUR OWN CITY FROM THE GOLDEN AGE BY DOWNLOADING FOLDING PAPERS FROM THE WEBSITE OF THE AMSTERDAM MUSEUM (SEE PAGE 57 AND AMSTERDAMMUSEUM.NL/BOUW-JE-EIGEN-STAD). GOOD LUCK!

IN THE 17TH CENTURY SPICES FROM ALL KINDS OF TROPICAL COUNTRIES WERE BEING STUDIED IN THE HORTUS BOTANICUS - THE BOTANICAL GARDEN OF AMSTERDAM (SEE PAGE 106). THE SPICES WERE IMPORTANT BECAUSE THEY WERE USED TO CURE DISEASES. DOCTORS AND PHARMACISTS HAD TO DO THEIR EXAMS IN THE HORTUS BOTANICUS.

The Decline

At the end of the 18th century Napoleon reigned in the Netherlands, as well as in Amsterdam. His brother Louis Napoleon Bonaparte became king and settled in the palace on Dam Square, which from that moment officially became a Royal Palace. The population got poorer and many people left the city. In 1864, the Vondelpark was laid out and nowadays it is hard to imagine that at that time the park was surrounded by meadows.

Central Station

The Reconstruction

In the 19th century the city expanded. More and more streets got paved and Central Station and the Carre theatre were built. Residents of Amsterdam could now no longer look over the IJ lake. During the First World War people in the city were starving. One day a large ship with potatoes intended for the soldiers arrived in the city harbour. Once people heard of the arrival they got so angry that they started protesting. They wanted those potatoes! In Amsterdam these protests are still known as the potato riots.

Theatre Carre

The Second World War

During this war people in the city were starving again. A lot of Jewish inhabitants (including Anne Frank) went into hiding, but many people still got arrested and were executed. After the war a large number of inhabitants moved to new neighbouring cities like Purmerend, Zaandam and Almere because they wanted more space. In that period many people from Suriname, Turkey and Morocco came to Amsterdam, because there was work to be done in the in the city that Dutch people didn't want to do themselves. Nowadays if you walk down the streets in Amsterdam, you will see people from all over the world.

HERE WE GO!

TOURIST INFORMATION

THE CENTRE

The city centre of Amsterdam is quite a large area. Of course this comprises Dam Square and the historic streets surrounding the square, but also the beautiful Jordaan, the Leidseplein and the famous Kalverstraat shopping street. Departing from Amsterdam Central Station most spots mentioned in this chapter can be easily reached on foot. So put on your walking shoes!

National Monument on Dam Square

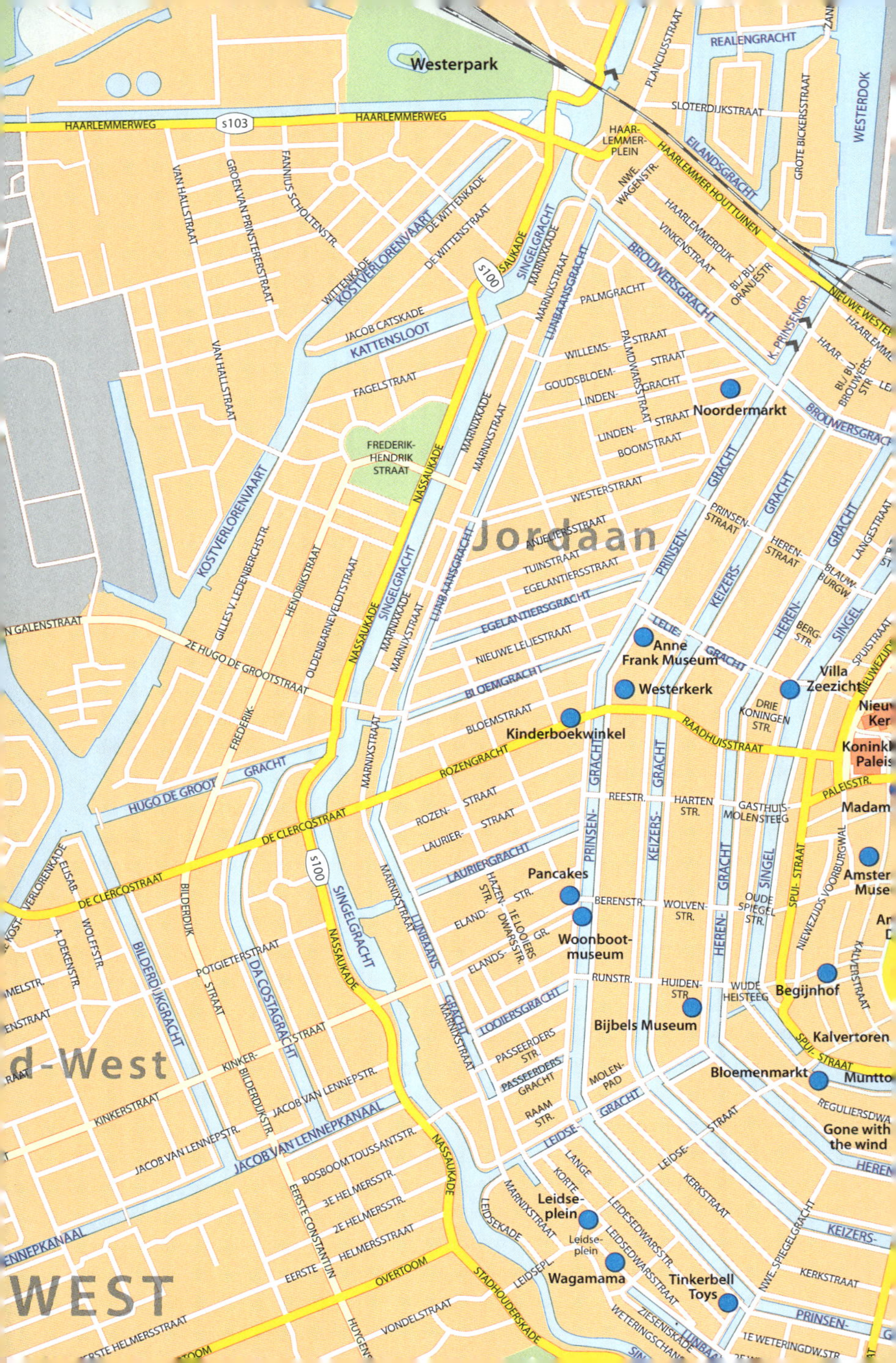
Westerpark
REALENGRACHT
WESTERDOK
HAARLEMMERWEG
s103
HAARLEMMERPLEIN
SLOTERDIJKSTRAAT
PLANCIUSSTRAAT
EILANDSGRACHT
GROTE BICKERSSTRAAT
HAARLEMMER HOUTTUINEN
HAARLEMMERDIJK
VINKENSTRAAT
NWE. WAGENSTR.
BROUWERSGRACHT
VAN HALLSTRAAT
GROEN VAN PRINSTERERSTRAAT
FANNIUS SCHOLTENSTR.
KOSTVERLORENVAART
DE WITTENKADE
DE WITTENSTRAAT
WITTENKADE
SAUKADE
SINGELGRACHT
MARNIXKADE
MARNIXSTRAAT
LIJNBAANSGRACHT
s100
JACOB CATSKADE
KATTENSLOOT
FAGELSTRAAT
PALMGRACHT
WILLEMSSTRAAT
GOUDSBLOEMSTRAAT
LINDENGRACHT
LINDENSTRAAT
BOOMSTRAAT
PALMDWARSSTRAAT
Noordermarkt
FREDERIK-HENDRIK STRAAT
NASSAUKADE
WESTERSTRAAT
Jordaan
ANJELIERSSTRAAT
TUINSTRAAT
EGELANTIERSSTRAAT
EGELANTIERSGRACHT
NIEUWE LELIESTRAAT
BLOEMGRACHT
BLOEMSTRAAT
PRINSENGRACHT
PRINSENSTRAAT
KEIZERSGRACHT
HERENSTRAAT
HERENGRACHT
BLAUWBURGW.
BERGSTR.
SINGEL
LANGESTRAAT
SPUISTRAAT
NIEUWEZIJDS
LELIEGRACHT
Anne Frank Museum
Westerkerk
Villa Zeezicht
DRIE KONINGEN STR.
Nieuwe Kerk
Koninklijk Paleis
Kinderboekwinkel
RAADHUISSTRAAT
PALEISSTR.
Madam
N GALENSTRAAT
2E HUGO DE GROOTSTRAAT
GILLES V. LEDENBERCHSTR.
HENDRIKSTRAAT
OLDENBARNEVELDTSTRAAT
FREDERIKSTRAAT
HUGO DE GROOTGRACHT
ROZENGRACHT
DE CLERCQSTRAAT
ROZENSTRAAT
LAURIERSTRAAT
LAURIERGRACHT
REESTR.
HARTENSTR.
GASTHUISMOLENSTEEG
Amsterdam Museum
KOST-VERLORENKADE
ELISABETH WOLFFSTR.
A. DEKENSTR.
BILDERDIJKGRACHT
BILDERDIJKSTRAAT
POTGIETERSTRAAT
DA COSTAGRACHT
SINGELGRACHT
Pancakes
Woonbootmuseum
BERENSTR.
WOLVENSTR.
OUDE SPIEGELSTR.
SPUISTRAAT
NIEUWEZIJDS VOORBURGWAL
KALVERSTRAAT
HAZENSTR.
ELANDSGRACHT
ELANDSSTR.
1E LOOIERSDWARSSTR.
LOOIERSGRACHT
RUNSTR.
HUIDENSTR.
WIJDE HEISTEEG
Begijnhof
Bijbels Museum
Kalvertoren
SPUISTRAAT
d-West
KINKERSTRAAT
JACOB VAN LENNEPSTR.
JACOB VAN LENNEPKANAAL
PASSEERDERSSTR.
PASSEERDERSGRACHT
MOLENPAD
RAAMSTR.
Bloemenmarkt
Munttoren
REGULIERSDWARSSTRAAT
Gone with the wind
BOSBOOM TOUSSAINTSTR.
3E HELMERSSTR.
2E HELMERSSTR.
HELMERSSTRAAT
EERSTE CONSTANTIJN HUYGENSSTRAAT
LEIDSEGRACHT
LEIDSESTRAAT
KERKSTRAAT
LANGE LEIDSEDWARSSTR.
KORTE LEIDSEDWARSSTR.
Leidseplein
LEIDSEKADE
NWE. SPIEGELSTRAAT
KEIZERSGRACHT
PRINSENGRACHT
HERENGRACHT
LEIDSEDWARSSTRAAT
Wagamama
Tinkerbell Toys
ZIESENISKADE
WETERINGSCHANS
LIJNBAANSGRACHT
1E WETERINGDW.STR.
ENNEPKANAAL
WEST
OVERTOOM
STADHOUDERSKADE
VONDELSTRAAT
LEIDSEPL.
EERSTE HELMERSSTRAAT

Het IJ
Centraal Station
St. Nicolaas-kerk
Schreierstoren
Oude Kerk
Oude Kerkspl.
Met. Deli
China Town
Nieuwmarkt
Zuiderkerk
Stadhuis
Mr. Visser Plein
Blauwbrug
Rembrandtplein
Tassenmuseum Hendrikje
Magere Brug
Theater Carré
Scheepvaart museum
Artis
Oosterdok
Java-
Tropenmuseu
N
OOST
De Ruijterkade
Piet Heinkade
Prins Hendrikkade
Damrak
Zeedijk
Geldersekade
Kromme Waal
Waals-Eilandsgracht
Binnenkant
Oude Waal
Recht Boomsloot
Krom Boomsloot
Kalkmarkt
Rapenburg
Oude Schans
Nwe. Uilenburgerstr.
Uilenburgergracht
Valkenburgerstraat
Anne Frankstr.
Foelie Dw. Str.
Rapenburgerstr.
Jodenbreestr.
Waterloopl.
Waterlooplein
Muiderstr.
Herengracht
Parklaan
Plantage
Plantage Kerklaan
Plantage Middenlaan
Plantage Muidergracht
Entrepotdok
Hoogte Kadijk
Laagte Kadijk
Nieuwe Vaart
Oostenburgergracht
Kattenburgerstraat
Dijksgracht
IJtunnel
Noordhollands-
Buiksloterweg
Meeuwenlaan
Spreeuwenpark
Gedempte Insteekhaven
Noordwal
Motorwal
Havikslaan
Adelaarsweg
Meidoornweg
Ranonkelkade
Tosaristraat
s100
s116
s113
Binnenamstel
Amstel
Nieuwe Keizersgracht
Nieuwe Prinsengracht
Nieuwe Herengracht
Nieuwe Achtergracht
Weesperstraat
Kerkstraat
Sarphatistraat
Mauritskade
Utrechtsestraat
Reguliersgracht
Kloveniersburgwal
Groenburgw.
Zwanenburgw.
O.Z. Voorburgwal
O.Z. Achterburgwal
Warmoesstraat
Beursstr.
Stormst.
L. Niezel
O. Brug Steeg
Bloed Str.
Barnde Steeg
Koningsstr.
Keizerstr.
Dijkstr.
St. Antonies Breestr.
O. Doelen Str.
Rusland
Singel
Grote Wittenburgerstraat
Kleine Wittenburgerstraat
Kattenburgergracht

THE ROYAL PALACE

location **Dam Square, 020 6204060, paleisamsterdam.nl** * **tram** **1, 2, 5, 13, 17 (stop Dam/ Raadhuisstraat), 4, 9, 16, 24 (stop Dam)** * **open** **variable dependent on royal receptions, check the website** * **admission** **€ 10, under 18 years free**

The people of Amsterdam call the Royal Palace also 'the Palace on Dam Square' because that is exactly where it is: on Dam Square. The palace was built in 1648, and originally it wasn't built as a palace but as a city hall. As you may have read in the story about the history of Amsterdam (see page 38), Dam Square is the heart of the historic city centre. So it was a pretty convenient spot for a city hall. And it was not just a regular city hall, the building was extremely big and beautiful considering the time in which it was constructed. Therefore, it was also called the eighth Wonder of the World. The construction costs were at least 8.5 million guilders (about 4 million euros)! The building stands on 13,659 wooden piles and inside the palace a lot of marble was used. The building was finished in 1665 and in that year it was officially taken into use.

City hall becomes a palace

Only when the French king Louis Napoleon Bonaparte started living in the building in 1808 did it get its royal status. From 1935 the palace is no longer owned by the city of Amsterdam, but by the State of the Netherlands and the State offered the royal family permanent use of the building. This does not mean that the king and queen live here. The palace is actually only used when important visitors come to the Netherlands or for parties and receptions of the royal family. King Willem-Alexander was crowned here in 2013. Visiting kings, queens and presidents from other countries also often stay at the palace. What a nice hotel!

Visiting

When the king or other members of the royal family do not use the palace it is open for the public, and most of the time that is the case. For families there is a (free) mobile guide available. Children aged 6-8 years can make a tour with prince Louis, the son of king Louis Napoleon. During this tour the prince will ask all kinds of questions and you can answer these questions by placing stickers on a special medallion. For children aged 9-12 there is the mystery Jacobs Adventure, which is set in the Golden Age. The story is very exciting and is especially for the palace written by the famous Dutch children's author Simon van der Geest. By listening carefully you will learn all about the history of this particular building.

DAM SQUARE IS AN ATTRACTION IN ITSELF. IT IS SWARMING WITH PIGEONS THAT JUST COME TO YOU AND EAT OUT OF YOUR HAND. THERE ARE ALSO MANY STREET ARTISTS AT WORK AND IN MAY AND OCTOBER YOU CAN GO TO THE FUN-FAIR AT DAM SQUARE.

TIP: GO FOR A DRINK TO THE ROOFTOP TERRACE OF THE BIJENKORF ON DAM SQUARE AND ENJOY A MAGNIFICENT VIEW OF THE CITY.

NATIONAL MONUMENT

location **Dam Square** * tram **4, 9, 16, 24 (stop Dam)**

In the picture at the beginning of this chapter you can see the National Monument on Dam Square. Children living in the Netherlands probably have seen it on television, at the annual national Remembrance of the Dead ceremony on the 4th of May. On that day king Willem-Alexander and queen Maxima lay a wreath at the memorial. The monument is the most important monument for the commemoration of World War II in the Netherlands and it was built in 1956. The monument consists of a concrete pillar 22 meters in height bearing a relief called 'Peace.' Let's see if you can discover it. On the front you can see four men with cuffs representing the sufferings during the war. The two men with howling dogs at their feet represent the resistance movement, and the pigeons that fly up at the back refer to the liberation. Above the central relief is a sculpture of a woman with a child in her arms and doves flying around her, representing victory, peace, and new life. Behind the pillar is a semi-circular, white wall with eleven urns, a kind of vases. The urns contain soil from the Dutch provinces and from the former Dutch East Indies.

Madame Tussauds

location 20 Dam Square, 020 5221010, madametussauds.com * tram 1, 2, 5, 17 and 20 (stop Magna Plaza/Dam), 4, 9, 16, 20, 24 and 25 (stop Bijenkorf/Dam). A 10 minute walk from Amsterdam CS * open daily 10 am -7 pm * admisison € 18, 5-15 years € 14

Fiona from the movie Shrek, President Obama, football player Rafael van der Vaart, Princess Beatrix and Robbie Williams. At Madame Tussauds you can meet all these celebrities, and you can have your picture taken with them. But how is that possible? The figures look exactly like real people but actually they are all made of wax. The work on a figure takes an average of three months and costs around 200,000 euros. Maybe you wonder why making a figure is so expensive. To begin with, all the figures are made in London. A celebrity first has to pose extensively and all his or her sizes are precisely recorded. There are also a lot of pictures taken. In the next phase a sculptor makes a statue of clay. He can make good use of the pictures to create a statue that is as lifelike as possible. The statue of clay is then used to make a plaster mould. In the next step the head and hands are made of wax, the rest of the body is made of fiberglass, which is much lighter than wax. Now it is time to dress up the figure, to colour the face and stick the hear on top of it. If the figure is ready, it is transported by a special driver to the ferry and then brought to Amsterdam. If you want to have a look inside Madame Tussauds you often have to stand in line. Our advice: ask your parents to buy tickets online in advance. This is not only cheaper, you are also allowed to use a special entrance and this goes a lot faster! Also good to know: there are special family prices and if you enter after 3 pm, this also saves money.

China Town

location Information Centre Amsterdam Oude Stad, 264 Nieuwezijds Voorburgwal, 020 6238622, amsterdamoudestad.nl * metro 51, 53, 54 (stop Nieuwmarkt) * open Mon-Fri 8.30 am - 5.30 pm

After a ten-minute walk from Amsterdam Central Station you arrive in the heart of China Town. This is the Chinese neighbourhood of Amsterdam, which is situated around the Geldersekade and the Zeedijk. In this neighbourhood you can find all kinds of Chinese shops, but also a Buddhist temple, Chinese markets and food stalls. Look closely at the street name signs: the names of the streets are written in both Chinese and in Dutch. The people in China Town celebrate all kinds of Chinese festivals such as Chinese New Year, with fireworks and a dragon dance (see the calendar of events on page 18). Maybe you have tried Chinese food before, noodles or Chinese crackers for example, but your grandparents probably did not eat Chinese food when they were your age. Only after World War II, around 1950, the Dutch and other Europeans started increasingly to enjoy Chinese food, which also increased the

Madame Tussauds

number of Chinese restaurants in Amsterdam, including those on the Zeedijk. Are you going to visit China Town? Of course you can just wander around a bit, but you can also pick up a free English map at the Information Centre Amsterdam Oude Stad showing you the best spots. The map can also be printed in advance via the website Amsterdamoudestad.nl.

TIP: AT THE INFORMATION CENTRE YOU CAN GET INFORMATION ON WALKING TOURS AND A QUEST THROUGH THIS OLD PART OF TOWN.

METROPOLITAN DELI

location **135 Warmoesstraat, 020 3301955, metropolitandeli.nl** * tram **4, 9, 16, 24 (stop Dam)** * open **daily from 9 am**

In the old town you will be delighted to discover Metropolitan Deli. It is a true chocolate paradise, but also an ice cream shop, espresso bar and dessert shop. Everything is homemade and we loved the sweet smell when we entered the shop. There are six different types of chocolate ice cream to choose from, so be prepared for a difficult choice.

Amsterdam Museum

location entrances: 92 Kalverstraat and 27 Sint Luciënsteeg, 020 5231822, amsterdammuseum.nl * tram 1, 2, 5 (stop Spui) * open daily 10 am - 5 pm * admission € 11, 5-18 years € 5

The former Amsterdam Historical Museum has been undergoing a facelift and therefore also got a new name: Amsterdam Museum. People who want to learn all about Amsterdam in less than an hour visit the exhibition Amsterdam DNA (with a free family tour. Also available in English). Discover all about the first inhabitants, the canals, the Golden Age, Ajax and the Red Light District. Do you want more? Then wander through the halls full of highlights from the history of Amsterdam.

The Little Orphanage

Het Kleine Weeshuis (the little orphanage) is an exhibition especially for children. Here you will discover in an exciting way the life in an orphanage in the 17th century. In this building the orphanage of the city of Amsterdam was housed for four centuries. Take a look in the dorms, classrooms and kitchens; watch an old loo and even a cowshed. You will experience these spaces with all your senses. Objects around you are whispering, you must hide from the residents, you learn penmanship and to milk cows. The little orphanage is also suitable for English speaking children.

© Amsterdam Museum

Amsterdam Dungeon

location 78 Rokin, 020 5308500, theamsterdamdungeon.nl * tram 4, 9, 16 and 24 (stop Spui/Rokin) * open every 15 minutes from 11 am - 5 pm a new tour; visit the website for opening hours during holidays * admission € 22, 5-15 years € 18, buying online tickets is cheaper

Do you want to learn more about the dark and scary history of Amsterdam? Then visit the Amsterdam Dungeon. With a group of up to thirty people you descend into the vaults of the Amsterdam Dungeon and watch 11 different shows with 9 actors and spectacular live effects. 'Murder on the Zeedijk' for example or 'Hell on the Batavia'. These shows are funny and educational at times, but also a bit scary. The actors performing in Amsterdam Dungeon really take you back in time and you will laugh and scream at the same time. According to the Amsterdam Dungeon website the attraction is suitable for children over ten years, but quite frankly we think this is still a bit young. It all depends on your own nerves! The tour lasts approximately 80 minutes. If you go to Amsterdam Dungeon and also want to visit the Rijksmuseum or Madame Tussauds please check the website for combination tickets. Buying tickets online saves money anyway.

© Amsterdam Dungeon

The Begijnhof

location **Begijnhof, 020 6221918, begijnhofamsterdam.nl** * **tram** **4, 9, 16 and 24 (stop Spui/ Rokin) or 1, 2 and 5 (stop Spui)** * **open** **daily 9 am - 5 pm** * **admission** **free**

Halfway through the Kalverstraat, at the Spui, you can visit the Begijnhof. Walk through the gate and marvel at the tranquillity of this courtyard. The houses around the lawn date from the 17th and 18th century, but the Begijnhof itself dates from the 14th century. In that time the Beguines lived here, religious women who cared for the sick. Beguines did not live in a monastery, but in a courtyard like this one. They had to obey the pastor and lead a religious life. But if they wanted to get married that was no problem, they just left the court. Look for the Houten Huys (No. 34). This was built in 1477 and is the oldest house in Amsterdam. In 1971 the last beguine died: sister Antonia. After her death the Begijnhof was completely renovated and nowadays there are 105 people living here. The residents are all single, Catholic women from thirty years and older. And yes, you are welcome to walk around, but try to be quiet.

THE 'HOUTEN HUYS' (MEANING 'WOODEN HOUSE') AT NO. 34 (LOOK AT THE PICTURE) WAS BUILT AROUND 1528 AND UNTIL 2012 PEOPLE THOUGHT THIS WAS THE OLDEST HOUSE IN AMSTERDAM. BUT IN THAT YEAR A CONTRACTOR DISCOVERED AN OLD WOODEN HOUSE HIDDEN BEHIND THE FACADE OF A HOUSE FROM THE 19TH CENTURY. THIS HOUSE IN THE WARMOESTRAAT WAS EVEN OLDER THAN THE HOUTEN HUYS AT THE BEGIJNHOF.

Le Pain Quotidien

location 266 Spuistraat, 020 6222555, lepainquotidien.nl * tram 4, 9, 16 and 24 (stop Spui/ Rokin), 1, 2 and 5 (stop Spui) * open daily 9 am - 6 pm

People who occasionally go to France are familiar with the wonderful Le Pain Quotidien. Currently there are four branches in Amsterdam, but in the nearby future more shops will be opened. Enjoy the generously filled organic sandwiches, but also the French toast and other goodies.

Flower Market

location Singel, between Koningsplein and Muntplein * tram 1, 2 and 5 (stop Koningsplein), 4, 9, 16, 24 (stop Muntplein) * open Mon-Sat 9 am - 5.30 pm, Sun 11 am - 5.30 pm

On the Singel you find one of the biggest tourist attractions of Amsterdam: the floating Flower Market. Both locals and tourists come here for their flowers, bulbs and plants. Since it is mostly very crowded at the market, stay close to your parents.

© Rob Gerritsen

THE FLOWER MARKET IS BUILT ON BOATS IN THE WATER BECAUSE IN THE OLD DAYS ALL THE FLOWERS WERE BROUGHT BY BOAT FROM OUTSIDE THE CITY. THIS MADE THE TRADE MUCH EASIER!

Juggle Store

location 3 Staalstraat, 020 4201980, juggle-store.com * tram 4, 9, 16 and 24 (stop Muntplein) * open Tue-Sat noon - 5.30 pm

Do you love the circus and street theatre? Then you definitely have to pay a visit to the Juggle Store. Here you can buy all kinds of stuff for your own circus act so when you get home you will have to start practicing. So choose a diabolo, hoop, or torche!

Blue

location 457 Singel, 020 4273901, blue-amsterdam.nl * tram 1, 2 and 5 (stop Koningsplein), 4, 9, 16 and 24 (stop Muntplein) * open Mon 11 am - 6.30 pm, Tue-Sat 10 am - 6.30 pm, Thu until 9 pm, Sun noon - 6.30 pm

On the third floor of the Kalvertoren shopping mall you can take a break at blue. From this heigth you have a stunning 360° view of the city and the restaurant is very suitable for children. Enjoy a yummy brunch with French toast or order a warm croissant with jam and butter. Also nice: the homemade lemonade and brownies. Or do you prefer a fresh orange juice with cheesecake? A difficult choice!

Calf & Bloom

location 461 Singel, 020 4228890, calfandbloom.nl * tram 1, 2 and 5 (stop Koningsplein), 4, 9, 16 and 24 (stop Muntplein) * open Mon 11 am - 8 pm, Tue-Sat 10 am - 8 pm, Thu until 10 pm, Sun noon - 8 pm

This is another good spot in the Kalvertoren shopping mall. Calf & Bloom is a nice restaurant for a drink, for breakfast or for lunch. When the weather is nice you can sit on the waterfront terrace at the Singelgracht. On the menu there are all kinds of children's favourites like chicken nuggets or tomato soup, but also bread with chocolate sprinkles. You can also try an English breakfast, order your own sorbet or one of the homemade sandwiches.

Gone with the Wind

location 22 Vijzelstraat, 020 4230230, gonewiththewind.nl * tram 4, 9, 16 and 24 (stop Muntplein) * open Mon noon - 6 pm, Tue-Sat 10 am - 6 pm, Sun noon - 5 pm

When you see the name of this shop, you do not immediately think of a toy store. Yet it is one and when you pay a visit you do not know where to start, because there are so many toys to choose from. The store is primarily intended for children up to eight years, but if you are older you will certainly still find something nice. At home you can already take a look in the online store to see what's for sale. We really adored the hundred different types of mobiles for your ceiling.

NeL

location 12 Amstelveld, 020 6261199, nelamstelveld.nl * tram 4 (stop Prinsengracht) * open daily from 10 am

The NeL restaurant is located on the Amstelveld and according to the owners this is the place to be for the most beautiful terrace in town. And we could not agree more! The terrace is certainly very spacious and has a children's playground and bowling alley. Sometimes there are musical performances that give you an instant holiday feeling. There are nice snacks on the menu, but you can also opt for lunch or dinner.

Tassenmuseum Hendrikje

location 572 Herengracht, 020 5246452, tassenmuseum.nl * tram 4 and 9 (stop Rembrandtplein), 16 and 24 (stop Keizersgracht), metro 51, 53 and 54 (stop Waterlooplein) * open daily 10 am - 5 pm * admission € 9,50, 13-18 years € 6, under 12 free

To be honest, the Tassenmuseum Hendrikje (museum of bags and purses) is perhaps more of a museum for girls than for boys. It is the largest museum of bags and purses in the world, with bags that originate from the year 1420 until now. Actually the museum started as a private bag collection of Hendrikje Ivo, who collcted bags for more than 35 years. Tassenmuseum Hendrikje teaches you all about 500 years of 'bag history'. It all begins with a goatskin bag from the 16th century and ends pretty much with the bag of Madonna. The museum is housed in a beautiful canal house from 1664 and in total you can admire more than 4,000 bags. Children from 8 to 12 years can go on a fun scavenger hunt through the museum with Natasja the Bags Detective and learn the story behind several extraordinary bags. Every last Saturday of the month a fun workshop is being organised for children over six years, where under supervision you can make a bag or pouch.

TASSEN
museum
HENDRIKJE

Biblical Museum

location 366 Herengracht, 020 6242436, bijbelsmuseum.nl * tram 1, 2 and 5 (stop Spui) * open Tue-Sat 10 am - 5 pm, Sun 11 am - 5 pm * admission € 8, 5-18 years € 4

The Biblical Museum (Bijbels Museum in Dutch) is housed in two beautiful houses at the Herengracht canal, and that alone makes the museum very special. In this museum you will learn stories from the Bible in all sorts of ways. Families can visit the exhibition 'Holiday! in the city' that is all about old stories and traditions. You will find the answers to questions like: Why is there no school at Easter? What do we celebrate then? And what other holidays do we celebrate? In the Museum Café you can enjoy tea with pastry from one of Amsterdam's renowned bakers with a view over the magnificent and peaceful museum garden.

© Bijbels Museum

Wagamama

location 10 Max Euweplein and 8 Amstelstraat, 020 5287778, wagamama.nl * tram Max Euweplein: 1, 2, 5, 7 and 10 (stop Leidseplein); Amstelstraat: 9 and 14 (stop Rembrandtplein) * open daily from noon

In this informal restaurant you can enjoy various noodle dishes. For children there is an extensive children's menu, with many dishes in smaller sized portions. What about fried chicken breast with Japanese rice or cucumber in a curry sauce? There are three branches in Amsterdam of which two are located in the city centre. The one on the Amstelstraat is just around the corner of the Rembrandtplein, the Max Euweplein is located near the Leidseplein. Enjoy!

TIP! DO YOU GO TO WAGAMAMA ON THE MAX EUWEPLEIN? THEN YOU CAN PLAY CHESS OUTSIDE ON A GIANT CHESS BOARD.

TINKERBELL TOYS

location 10-12 Spiegelgracht, 020 6258830, tinkerbelltoys.nl * tram 1, 2 and 5 (stop Prinsengracht) * open Mon 1 pm - 6 pm, Tue-Sat 10 am - 6 pm, Sun noon - 5 pm

This toy store sells mainly educational toys. Boring? No, not at all! It is fun to have a toy that has to do with light, construction, nature, electricity or movement. We loved the microscoop-set and the kit for a solar house. But maybe you prefer a clock with native songbirds, a backpack to go hiking in nature, an aromatic bomb to put in your bath or a box for experimenting with mixing colours.

FROZZ

location 27 Utrechtsestraat, 06 81883869, frozz.com * tram 1, 2 and 5 (stop Keizersgracht) * open normally noon - 9 pm, but check Facebook for the exact opening hours

Do you fancy something cold and fresh? Then go to Frozz. In this ice cream shop you can eat frozen yoghurt with all kinds of delicious things on top. So no plain yoghurt, but icy Dutch yoghurt freezed on the spot. Make a choice between nuts, fresh fruit, chocolate chips or any other delcicious treat and enjoy! There are currently four branches in Amsterdam, including this one, and one on the fifth floor of the Bijenkorf department store on Dam Square.

DE TAART VAN M'N TANTE

location 10 Ferdinand Bolstraat, 020 7764600, detaart.com * tram 16 and 24 (stop Stadhouderskade) * open daily 10 am - 6 pm

De Taart van m'n Tante (The Cake of my Aunt in English) is a short walk from Rembrandt Square, in the Pijp. This is one of the most famous cake shops in Amsterdam, and probably in the Netherlands. The reason is that one of the owners is Siemon de Jong, a Dutch television host. De Taart van m'n Tante is a bakery where you can order a very special (birthday) cake but it is also a cheerful 'Konditorei' where you can try a lot of delicious sweets.

Houseboat Museum

location 296-K Prinsengracht, 020 4270750, houseboatmuseum.nl * tram 1, 2 and 5 (stop Spui), 13 and 17 (stop Westermarkt) * open variable, check the website for opening hours * admission € 3,75, 5-15 years € 3

There are a lot of houseboats in the Netherlands. The city of Amsterdam has quite a record with 2500 of these houses on water. The Houseboat Museum (Woonbootmuseum in Dutch) is located in the 'Hendrika Maria', a former freighter moored on the Prinsengracht. Until the 1960s, the boat was primarily used for hauling sand and gravel. Even after it was turned into a houseboat, the owners kept much of its original exterior. A lot of people are a bit curious as to what a houseboat looks like from the inside. How do the residents get water for example? And is it very dark and damp? Vincent van Loon lives in a houseboat and he had to answer these questions all the time. That is why in 1997 he opened the Houseboat Museum. This specific houseboat has a size of about 80 m2, which is as big as an average apartment in Amsterdam. If your parents want to look around longer than you, just start looking for the play area for children.

De Taart van m'n Tante

The Westertower

PANCAKES AMSTERDAM

location 38 Berenstraat, 020 5289797, pancakesamsterdam.com * tram 1, 2 and 5 (stop Spui), 13 and 17 (stop Westermarkt) * open daily 10 am - 7 pm

A lot of people in the Netherlands think that a pancake is a typical Dutch treat. But maybe you know from experience that pancakes are also eaten in other countries, but every country has its own way of preparing them. In Russia they eat blinis for example, and in America fluffy American pancakes. At Pancakes! Amsterdam they know all the different recipes, and you can choose from a wide variety of pancakes. From a traditional Dutch pancake with apple to a Turkish version with dill, mint and feta. Or how about a savory French crepe with cheese, spinach and ham? The menu changes four times a year. And did you not have breakfast this morning? Try the delicious Pancakes!-breakfast.

ON THE 5TH OF JUNE 1806 KING LOUIS NAPOLEON BONAPARTE - THE BROTHER OF THE FAMOUS EMPEROR NAPOLEON BONAPARTE - INTRODUCED PANCAKE DAY IN THE NERTHERLANDS BECAUSE HE WAS VERY FOND OF PANCAKES. WRITE THAT DATE ON YOUR CALENDAR!

WESTERTOWER

location 281 Prinsengracht, 020 6892565, westertorenamsterdam.nl * tram 13, 14 and 17 (stop Westermarkt) * open climbing the tower from Apr-Oct, look at the website for opening hours * admission € 7,50, under 6 years free

The Westerkerk church, also called the Old Wester, is located almost next to the Anne Frank Museum. The church has the highest church tower in Amsterdam (85 meters, 87 meters if you count the cock) and we mention this tower here because in summer you can climb all the way to the top. This takes you 190 steps, but then you have a beautiful view of the city and you can even see the annex of Anne Frank from here. The carillon of the Westerkerk is equally impressive. This consists of 50 bells weighing in total more than 20,000 pounds. You can here the carillon every Tuesday between noon and 1 pm.

ON TOP OF THE TOWER YOU CAN SEE A CROWN. IN THE PICTURE THIS CROWN IS GOLD BUT NOWADAYS IT IS PAINTED IN BLUE. BLUE WAS THE ORIGINAL COLOUR.

Anne Frank Museum

location 263-267 Prinsengracht, 020 5567100, annefrank.org * tram 13, 14, 17 or bus 170, 172, 174 (stop Westermarkt) * open 15 Sep-14 Mar daily 9 am - 7 pm (Sat until 9 pm); 15 Mar-14 Sep daily 9 am - 9 pm (Sat until 10 pm), Jul and Aug daily until 10 pm * admission € 9, children € 4,50, under 10 years free

In World War II there was a girl who kept a diary from her hiding place in Amsterdam. This girl was named Anne Frank and both she and her diary are still famous all around the world. And no wonder, because people who have read the book will agree that it is very impressive to experience the war through the eyes of a child. For those who do not exactly know who Anne Frank was: this German Jewish girl was 4 years old when she came with her parents to the Netherlands, fleeing from the Nazis. The family first lived in the south of Amsterdam, but when it became too dangerous in 1942, she went into hiding on the Prinsengracht. They moved into the rear of a commercial building and the entrance of the secret annex was hidden behind a bookcase. Here they lived for two years, after which they were betrayed and arrested. The family was deported to a concentration camp, where only father Otto survived the war. The house where Anne Frank went into hiding is today one of the most visited tourist attractions of the city. In the front is an exhibition featuring many objects from the hiding period. After visiting this exhibition, go to the back part of the house where the Secret Annex was located. Especially the pictures of old movie stars on the wall of Anne's bedroom make a big impression. The first film that is shown in the Anne Frank Museum contains images of concentration camps that could be shocking for children.

Door to the secret annex

TIP! OFTEN THERE ARE LONG QUEUES AT THE MAIN ENTRANCE. BUYING TICKETS ONLINE ALLOWS YOU TO ENTER THROUGH A SPECIAL ENTRANCE TO THE LEFT OF THE MAIN ENTRANCE.

TIP! AFTER YOUR VISIT YOU CAN RENT A CANAL BIKE. A RENTAL PIER IS LOCATED IN FRONT OF THE MUSEUM. SEE PAGE 31 FOR MORE INFORMATION.

VILLA ZEEZICHT

location **7 Torensteeg, 020 6267433** * **tram** **1, 2, 5, 13 and 17 (stop Dam/Raadhuisstraat)** * **open** **daily 9 am - 9.30 pm**

Famous in Amsterdam: the freshly baked apple pie at the Villa Zeezicht café. In summer there is a lovely terrace at the canal, and in winter you sit cosy inside the centuries old building. Also try one of the sandwiches, toasted sandwiches or homemade soup. They are all equally delicious.

THE OLD DUTCH CANDY SHOP

Location **2 Tweede Egelantierdwarsstraat, 020 4207390, snoepwinkeltje.com** * **tram** **1, 2 and 5 (stop Dam), 13 and 17 (stop Westermarkt)** * **open** **Tue-Sat 11 am - 6.30 pm**

Visit this shop near the Anne Frank Museum and you immediately know everything there is to know about the history of Dutch candy. The owner Mariska not only sells dozens of different kinds of candy, she also knows everything about them. She learned the trade from her grandmother who already sold candy in Amsterdam. Try licorice, cinnamon sticks and black and white powder (all typically Dutch sweets). We love the jodenvet also called borsthoning. This treat consists of hard white lumps that initially have no flavor, but if you leave them in your mouth for a while they become nice and sweet at first, then bitter. Mariska also sells sugar-free candy, and through the webshop you can order everything that is on sale in the store.

ON THE WEBSITE OF THE SHOP YOU CAN FIND NICE COLORING PICTURES AND INTERESTING INFORMATION FOR A SCHOOL PRESENTATION.

NOORDERMARKT

location **Noordermarkt** * **bus** **18, 21, 22 (stop Buiten Brouwersstraat)**

Do you like to browse through secondhand stuff and old books? Then go vistit the flea market at the Noordermarkt in the Jordaan on Monday morning. On Saturdays this market place turns into a farmers market where you can taste all kinds of goodies. From Central Station it is a 20-minute walk to the Noordermarkt and you will cross the Haarlemmerstraat with all sorts of fun little shops. At the Noordermarkt itself there are several restaurants and cafes. If you like apple pie Winkel 43 is a must.

THE GAMEKEEPER

location **14 Hartenstraat, 020 6381579, gamekeeper.nl** * **tram** **1, 2, 5, 13 and 17 (stop Dam)** * **open** **Mon and Sat 10 am - 6 pm, Tue, Wed, Fri 10 am - 6.30 pm, Thu until 8.30 pm, Sun 11 am - 6 pm**

Do you love to play board games? At The Gamekeeper they have more than thousand board games in stock. From the more mainstream ones like Risk, Monopoly and Yahtzee to special board games. Feel free to ask for advice, because the people who work here also love to play games. You can also buy all kinds of jigsaw puzzles. From starters puzzles with four pieces to difficult ones with 24,000 pieces. These keep you busy for a couple of weeks!

Noorder Playground

location 10 2e Lindendwarsstraat, 020 6231256, vereniging-de-noorderspeeltuin.nl * bus 18 and 21 (stop Nieuwe Willemstraat), bus 22 (stop Buiten Oranjestraat)

Even in the city centre there are playgrounds, but sometimes only insiders know where to find them. The Noorder Playground (Noorderspeeltuin in Dutch) is located in the Jordaan. It also has a clubhouse and older children can have a great time on the (football) field. Smaller children will like the swings and the playing in the sand.

The Children's Bookstore

location 34 Rozengracht, 020 6224761, kinderboekwinkel.nl * tram 13 and 17 (stop Westermarkt) * open Mon 1-6 pm, Tue-Fri 10 am - 6 pm, Sat 10 am - 5 pm

Do you like to read? Then take a look at the Children's Bookstore (Kinderboekwinkel in Dutch) selling around 7,000 different books. Obviously most books are written in Dutch, but there are also some English books on offer. The store was the first children's bookstore in the Netherlands and exists around forty years.

Jordino

locatie 25A Haarlemmerdijk, 020 4203225, jordino.nl * on foot from Central Station * open Sun-Mon 1-6.30 pm, Tue-Sat 10 am - 6.30 pm

Yummy, yummy, yummy. In amsterdam (and beyond!) Jordino is known for its delicious ice cream, but also for its chocolates, cakes and cream truffles. What about pear-chocolate cake, butter cake with Italian almond paste and a hundred and fifty different ice flavors?

Monte Pelmo

locatie 17 2e Anjeliersdwarsstraat, 020 6230959, montepelmo.nl * tram 13 and 17 (stop Westermarkt), bus 18 (stop Marnixplein) * open daily 1-10 pm

In the fifties Monte Pelmo started as a snack bar but it soon turned out that the chefs were also very good at making ice cream, and that is what they are still doing today. In winter all kinds of new flavors are developed that you can taste the next summer. Useful for children with allergies: on the website you can not only see which flavors you can choose from, but also whether they contain cow's milk, gluten, peanuts or egg.

AROUND THE IJ LAKE & NORTH AMSTERDAM

The IJ lake is Amsterdam's waterfront and it is situated behind Amsterdam Central Station. Once the IJ was a bay of the Zuiderzee and nowadays you can cross the water with one of the free ferries. You will arrive in North Amsterdam where you can visit quite a few interesting spots. Maybe you also want to go to IJburg. This is a new suburb of Amsterdam located on islands created in the IJ.

The inner court of the National Maritime Museum

Pllek
Noorderlicht
IJ-kantine
Pannenkoekenboot
IJscuypje
Het IJ
EYE
Tolhuistuin
Centraal Station
St. Nicolaas-kerk
Ronde Lutherse Kerk
Schreiers-toren
OBA
NEMO
OOSTER-DOK
Klanksp
Hanneke
Oude Kerk
Nieuwe Kerk
Koninklijk Paleis
Dam
CENTRUM
WESTERDOK
DISTELWEG
GRASWEG
TOLHUISKANAAL
ASTERWEG
BUIKSLOTERKANAAL
BUIKSLOTERWEG
J. VAN HASSELTKANAAL-WEST
PAPAVERWEG
DISTELKADE
MOSPLEIN
JOHAN VAN
MOSVELD
RIBESSTR.
HAGEDOORNWEG
VAN DER PEKSTRAAT
RANONKELKADE
MEIDOORNWEG
NOORDHOLLANDS-
s116
SPREEUWENPARK
MEEUWENLAAN
GEDEMPTE INSTE
IJTUNNEL
DE RUIJTERKADE
s100
SINGEL
PRINS HENDRIKKADE
WESTERDOKSDIJK
NIEUWE WESTERDOKSTR.
HAARLEMMER HOUTTUINEN
LEMMERSTRAAT
BROUWERSGRACHT
GROTE BICKERSSTRAAT
ZANDHOEK
K. PRINSENGR.
NIEUWENDIJK
DAMRAK
ZEEDIJK
GELDERSEKADE
KROMME WAAL
WAALS-EILANDSGRACHT
OUDE WAAL
BINNENKANT
KALK-MARKT
RAPENBURG
NIEUW-MARKT
SCHANS
SPUISTRAAT
NIEUWEZIJDS VOORBURGWAL
LANGESTRAAT
KORSJES-POORT STEEG
BEURSSTR.
WARMOESSTRAAT
ST. JANSSTR.
O.Z. VOORBURGWAL
O.Z. ACHTERBURGWAL
OUDE KERKSPL.
STORMST.
L. NIEZEL
PALEISSTR.
KALVERSTRAAT
ROKIN
DAMSTR.
PIJLSTEEG
P. JABOBSZ STR.
O. DOELEN STR.
BARNDE STEEG
BLOED STR.
KONINGSSTR.
KEIZERSSTR.
DIJKSTR.
KROM BOOMSLOOT
RECHT BOOMSLOOT
ST. ANTONIES BRE
FOELIE DW. STR.

Noord
W.H. Vliegenbos
Het IJ
IJburg
Pampus
Firma Koek
Java-eiland
Jan
Schaeferbrug
Magazzino
IJhaven
KNSM-eiland
Keet in Huis
Oostelijk
Havengebied
Ertshave
Oostelijke
Handelskade
Sporenburg
Borneo-eila
Grote
Die
Grote
Haven
Noordhollandskanaal
Nieuwe Leeuwarderweg
Leeuwardenweg
Waddenweg
Walcherenstr.
Waddendijk
Rode Kruisstraat
Nieuwe Purmerweg
Purmerweg
Nieuwendammerdijk
Nieuwendammerkade
Zijkanaal naar
Nieuwendam
Adelaarsweg
Johan van
Meeuwenlaan
Zamenhofstraat
Hasseltweg
Schaatsstr.
Motorwal
Sumatrakade
Javakade
Tosaristraat
Verbindingsdam
KNSM-laan
Piet Heinkade
Oostelijke Handelskade
Van Hengelstra
Panamakade
Piet Hein
Stuurmankade
Borneolaan
C. van Heesterenlaan
Panamalaan
Kattenburgervaart
Burgerstraat
Wittenburgervaart
s116
s100

PUBLIC LIBRARY

location 143 Oosterdokskade, 020 5230900, oba.nl * on foot a few minutes walk from Amsterdam Central Station * open daily 10 am - 10 pm * admission free

The Amsterdam Public Library (OBA) has its headquarters on the Oosterdok near Amsterdam Central Station. Perhaps you wonder why tourists should pay a visit to a library, as they are not allowed to borrow books. But this not just a library. The OBA is also known for its many nice restaurants. Go to the roof terrace on the top floor and you will have a beautiful view over the city. Also worth your while: a visit to The Mouse House. Dutch children love this house because it features in the famous Dutch children's book The Mouse House by Karina Schaapman. The house is almost two meters wide, three meters high, and has more than a hundred rooms. Say hello to the mouse family when you see them!

HANNEKES BOOM

location 4 Dijksgracht, 020 4199820, hannekesboom.nl * tram 25 and 26 (stop Muziekgebouw aan het IJ) * open daily from 11 am

Opposite the Nemo science museum (see page 80) you will find Hannekes Booms, a quaint restaurant serving a delicious sustainable lunch, a (late) breakfast and other tasty food. You sit at the waterfront, but a picnic in the nearby park or on the boat is also possible. The menu changes quite often and children can participate in all kinds of crafts. So what are you waiting for?

The National Maritime Museum

location I Kattenburgerplein, 020 5232222, hetscheepvaartmuseum.nl * bus 22 and 48 (stop Kadijksplein) * open daily 9 am - 5 pm * admission € 15, 5-17 years € 7,50

A few years ago The National Maritime Museum (Het Scheepvaartmuseum in Dutch) was completely renovated and now it is one of the best museums in Amsterdam. The maritime history of the Netherlands, and in particular of the East India Companies, is explained by interactive exhibitions. This makes a visit not only educational, but also very entertaining.

Children's shows

There are several children's exhibitions for various ages. The youngest children (under 6 years) take a look into the magical underwater world of 'Sal & Lori and Circus at Sea'. Older children learn everything about whales in 'The tale of the whale' or they can experience a virtual adventure in wild waves and storms in the exciting ride 'Voyage at Sea'. Children aged 10 to 14 years discover the multimedia exhibition 'See you in the Golden Age'.

The ship

Outside at the quay of the museum you can find a famous replica of the 17th century ship The Amsterdam. In the 17th century, also called the Golden Age, the Netherlands were one of the richest and most powerful countries in the world. This was mainly due to the trade with the Far East and no other country had as many ships as the Netherlands. With those ships a lot of expensive goods were transported to Amsterdam. In Amsterdam they were sold again to other European countries. In the ship outside the museum you can see some furnished rooms and learn how people used to live aboard the ship.

THE SHIP 'THE AMSTERDAM' WAS BUILT IN 1748 AND A YEAR LATER IT SET SAIL FOR THE VERY FIRST TIME. THE CREW CONSISTED OF 203 MEN AND APART FORM THEM THERE WERE 127 SOLDIERS AND 5 PASSENGERS ON BOARD. IN THE HOLD WERE 27 BOXES OF SILVER WITH A WORTH OF UP TO 120,000 EUROS.

The Sound Playground

location 1 Piet Heinkade, 020 7882000, muziekgebouw.nl/jeugd * tram 26 (stop Muziekgebouw) * open Wed and Sun afternoon, 3 pm - 4.30 pm * admission € 8,50

In the Sound Playground (Klankspeeltuin in Dutch) at the Muziekgebouw aan 't IJ music hall you can experiment with several sound installations. These are a kind of music machines. and on each machine you can make music. Take the Xenax for example, with which you can draw sounds. The Omni is a musical mushroom that you can play with your hands. The sound installations can be used every Wednesday and Sunday. During the workshop (for children aged 7 years and older) your parents are not around. They can have a drink downstairs at the Restaurant Zouthaven. Or better yet: let them go to a concert, because often that is possible at the same time. Afterwards they will come to your concert.

Nemo

location 2 Oosterdok, 020 5313233, e-nemo.nl * bus 22 and 48 (stop Kadijksplein) * open Tue-Sun 10 am - 5.30 pm, Mai-Aug daily during all offical school holidays * admission € 15, under 3 years free

This great technology and science museum is located next to the National Maritime Museum. You can visit exhibitions but also perform a lot of scientific experiments. In the Wonder Lab

The National Maritime Museum

The Amsterdam

© Jurjen Drenth Photography

NEMO

© DigiDaan

Roof terrace NEMO

© DigiDaan

for example, you may recolor red cabbage or make glue out of potatoes. But in the rest of the museum are also plenty of activities to be found. Experiment with hydropower, build a solid bridge or tower and step into an elevator for a dizzying experience.

Chain Reaction

The absolute hit are the soap bubbles on the first floor. Ask you parents for a hand and get locked in your own bubble. Several times a day an interesting chain reaction is demonstrated on this floor including moving office chairs, popping balloons and falling bricks. In 'Codename: DNA' you can make a trip through your body and 'Smart Technology' focuses on sustainable technology.

Roof terrace

On the roof of NEMO you will find the largest roof terrace in all Amsterdam, 22 metres above water level. Enjoy a splendid view of the city centre, play a game of giant chess, and if the weather is nice you can play in the interactive water feature. There is also a nice café and plenty of space to sit back and relax. The roof terrace is freely accessible, either by climbing the 120 steps to the top or by taking the elevator from NEMO's entrance hall. There are plans to develop a (free) open-air exhibition on the roof.

SOMETIMES YOU CAN SEE A HUGE VEHICLE PLUNGING INTO THE WATER NEAR NEMO. THIS IS THE FLOATING DUTCHMAN, A TOURIST BUS THAT JUST DRIVES INTO THE WATER. FOR MORE INFORMATION ABOUT THIS ATTRACTION SEE PAGE 30.

THERE IS ALSO A NEMO BRANCH AT SCHIPHOL AIRPORT. HERE YOU CAN SEE THE KUNDT TUBE FOR EXAMPLE THAT MAKES INVISIBLE SOUND WAVES VISIBLE. THERE ARE ALSO SPECIAL MIRRORS AND YOU CAN FILL IN A COMPUTER QUESTIONNAIRE TO DETERMINE YOUR OWN UNIQUENESS. NEMO SCHIPHOL IS LOCATED IN AIRPORT PARK, AT THE BEGINNING OF PIER D.

MAGAZZINO

location 19 Jollemanhof, 020 4198978, magazzinoamsterdam.nl * tram 26 (stop Kattenburgerstraat) * open Mon-Fri from 11 am, Sat + Sun from 5 pm

This restaurant is located on the Eastern Docklands in Pakhuis Africa (a former warehouse). This is a very special spot with a nice terrace. There is no children's menu, but we have been told that the chefs can prepare something on request for children.

The Pancake Boat

location Ms. van Riemsdijkweg (departure), 020 6368817, pannenkoekenboot.nl/amsterdam * ferry behind Central Station to NDSM-werf, bus 91 or 94 from behind Central Station (stop Klaprozenweg) * open see the website for departure times * admission from € 15,75, 3-12 years € 11,25

We think all children would love to make a canal cruise and meanwhile eat as many traditional Dutch pancakes as they like. It can be done on the Pancake Boat (Pannenkoekenboot in Dutch). There are various tours, including the 75-minute cruise across the IJ and the Family Cruise lasting 2 ½ hours. On the decoration table there are all sorts of yummy things for designing your own pancake. You can also colour at your table and in the hold is a ball bath with 15,000 coloured balls. The boat departs from North Amsterdam. To get there you take the (free) ferry behind Amsterdam Central Station to the NDSM-werf. The Pancake Boat is located at the pier of the ferry.

Museum Werf 't Kromhout

location 147 Hoogte Kadijk, 020 627677, kromhoutmotorenmuseum.nl * bus 48 (stop Kadijksplein) * open Tue 10 am - 3 pm

The Kromhout Shipyard is one of the oldest shipyards in Amsterdam. If you like boats this is an interesting place to visit. In the 1970s the City Council of Amsterdam wanted to get rid of the shipyard but a lot of people wanted to save it and started protesting. Now it is back into use and on Tuesdays the general public can have a look at the Shipyard Museum. The museum is located in an old factory and gives you quite an idea of the history of shipbuilding. Also on display: an interesting collection of steam engines and motors, and (old) tools. Around the yards are many ships to admire.

Keet in Huis

location 297 KNSM-laan, 020 4195958, keetinhuis.nl * bus 48 (stop Azartplein) or tram 26 (stop Rietlandpark) * open Tue-Sat 10 am - 6 pm, Sun noon - 5 pm

Keet in Huis is a beautiful shop selling great stuff, and we are sure that especially your mum will really enjoy it. You have come to the right place for clothing, furniture and all sorts of fun gadgets for kids. Keet in Huis also sells the popular Dutch clothing brand Imps & Elfs and the entire collection is in stock. Other brands include KidsCase, Falke, Bergstein, Petit Bateau and American Outfitters. An insider's tip: look for the furniture of Dutch designer Piet Hein Eek.

IJburg

IJburg is a special residential area in Amsterdam. Every year this neighbourhood gets bigger and bigger and each time it takes up more of the IJ lake. Maybe you are wondering how that is possible. The city of Amsterdam creates artificial islands in the water on which houses are being built. There are already three such islands (Steigereiland, Haveneiland and Rietlanden), and eventually there will be seven. At present IJburg is considered to be the most child friendly district of Amsterdam and there are quite some fun things to do.

Vrijburcht

location 159 Jan Olphert Vaillantlaan, 020 4165005, vrijburcht.nl * tram 26 (stop Steigereiland) * open café: Tue-Fri from 3 pm, Sat-Sun from noon

At Vrijburcht on IJburg you can enjoy a theatre show or a snack and a drink. Better yet: do both and make sure you have a fun outing. In the small theatre you van watch all kinds of children's shows and movies, puppet shows and children's concerts. In the café you can order a delicious sandwich, or - even better - order several appetizers and eat them on the lovely terrace overlooking the water.

BLIJBURG

IJburg has its own beach, Blijburg, that is constantly on the move as the neighbourhood expands. See page 149 for the current location of Blijburg.

IJBURG CONSISTS OF SEVERAL ISLANDS, SO NO WONDER THAT THERE ARE MANY BRIDGES ON IJBURG. BETWEEN THE ZEEBURGEREILAND AND THE STEIGEREILAND YOU CAN FIND ONE OF THE LARGEST BRIDGES IN AMSTERDAM. OFFICIALLY IT IS CALLED THE ENNE'S HEERMA BRIDGE BUT RESIDENTS OF IJBURG CALL IT 'THE BRA'. LOOK AT THE PICTURE ABOVE. WHAT DO YOU THINK?

DIEMERPARK

location oost.amsterdam.nl * tram 26 (stop Diemerparklaan or Zuiderzeeweg)

The Diemerpark is located at the border of IJburg. This park exists since 2004 and was previously a landfill. Now you can go hiking, biking, and rollerblading in the park, but you can also play golf. When the weather is nice there is even a beach. Insider's tip: find the water wells and admire the beautiful paintings that artists have made on it. Boring gray concrete wells have become tiny works of art.

Bloem

location 1289 IJburglaan, 020 4160677, bloemopijburg.nl * tram 26 (stop Diemerparklaan) * open daily from 5 pm

On the Bloem website it is stated clearly: children are welcome! So we went to this Italian restaurant and enjoyed their delicious pizzas. The pizzas are all prepared in a wood-fired oven and besides pizza, there are all kinds of other wonderful things on the menu. It is worth mentioning that this menu changes every day. In summer you can sit outside on the terrace or opt for take-away. Buy your pizza, antipasti or meal of the day and find a nice spot on IJburg for a lovely picnic.

MAYBE YOU HAVE NOTICED THAT A LOT OF THE MENTIONED SHOPS AND RESTAURANTS ARE LOCATED ON THE IJBURGLAAN. THIS STREET IS THE MAIN STREET OF IJBURG AND CONNECTS THE ISLANDS ZEEBURGEREILAND, STEIGEREILAND AND HAVENEILAND. TRAM NO. 26 RUNS FROM AMSTERDAM CENTRAL STATION ALL ALONG THE IJBURGLAAN. THAT IS VERY CONVENIENT!

Shopping

On IJburg there is plenty of shopping to do. Go to IJgenwijs for example (1285 IJburglaan) for fun and unusual gifts or to Lightning & Stars (1153 IJburglaan) for clothes and shoes for children aged 2 to 14 years. Another tip: Flo 4 Kidz, where they sell everything for children up to ten years such as clothing, shoes, accessories, gifts and much more. *IJgenwijs.nl, Bliksemensterren.nl, Flo4kidz.nl*

Fortress Island Pampus

location 0294 262326, pampus.nl * open departure (from the port of IJburg) Apr 5 - Oct 26 Tue-Fri 11 am, Sat + Sun 11 am and 1.30 pm * admission ferry + admission € 20, 4-11 years € 15

Look around in the port of IJburg and take the ferry to Fortress Island Pampus. This island was built over 100 years ago and was intended to protect Amsterdam against hostile invaders. Fortress Island Pampus is situated in the IJ lake between Amsterdam and Muiden and you can visit the island by using the ferry. The boat trip and the visit of the fortress take

The ferry to fortress island Pampus

Adventurous Pampus

© Gerke van der Hoef

about four hours, and when it rains this is no problem since both the ferry and the fortress island have a roof. In total you have 2 ½ hours to entertain yourself on the island. This might sound as a long time, but take it from us: time flies. You can take a guided tour, there are games hidden in the fortress and thanks to the quests you learn anything about the fort and its surroundings. In the Pampus Pavilion you can relax and have something to eat and drink.

IN DUTCH WE HAVE AN EXPRESSION THAT SAYS 'LYING IN FRONT OF PAMPUS'. WE USE IT FOR PEOPLE WHO ARE IN A DEEP SLEEP OR ARE VERY DRUNK. THE EXPRESSION REFERS TO THE OLD DAYS WHEN THE SHIPS LAY WAITING FOR GOOD WIND IN FRONT OF THE FORTRESS ISLAND PAMPUS. THE CREW HAD NOTHING TO DO AND COULD ONLY RELAX AND SLEEP.

FIRMA KOEK

location 404-406 Krijn Taconiskade, 020 7712554, firmakoek.nl * tram 26 (stop IJburg) * open daily from noon - 9 pm

Firma Koek (the Cooky Company in English) is located in the port of IJburg and it is a good place for yummy pancakes. It is not necessary to make a reservation, just walk in and order something tasty from the menu. Whether you want a traditional Dutch pancake with sugar, a very sweet one with ice cream, a savory goat cheese pancake or a vegetable one: it's all possible. You don't fancy pancakes? Try the flammkuchen. Flammkuchen? Yes, this is a kind of thin pizza crusts, smeared with crème fraîche with a topping of prawns, chorizo or bacon and egg.

IN LOCK 2008 - THE FIRST LOCK OF IJBURG - THERE IS A HIPPO IN THE WATER. THIS ARTWORK WAS CREATED BY THE ARTIST TOM CLAASSEN. DEPENDING ON THE WATER LEVEL YOU CAN SEE THE HIPPO COMPLETELY OR PARTIALLY. THE HIPPOPOTAMUS IS 6 BY 3 METERS WIDE AND MADE OF A SPECIAL RUBBER. TOM CLAASSEN HAS MADE OTHER FAMOUS ANIMAL ARTWORKS IN THE NETHERLANDS. AT THE CITY OF ALMERE THERE ARE FIVE HUGE ELEPHANTS STANDING ALONGSIDE THE HIGHWAY A6.

North Amsterdam

Not so long ago the north of Amsterdam was not a very attractive part to visit. But that has changed! Nowadays there is plenty to do in 'Noord' - as the locals call it. The nice thing about North Amsterdam is that you have to cross the IJ lake to get there. You do this by taking one of the free ferries and this is a lot of fun.

A little bit of history

It might be interesting to know that in the last century there were many large companies in North Amsterdam, especially in the field of shipbuilding and manufacturing. The people working there lived in the neighbourhoods around the factories. Since the late 1960s the industry has almost completely vanished, but you will still see many buildings from that period of time. Shipyards for example, or large cranes. Many old factory buildings are now used as offices for advertising agencies and state-of-the-art companies like MTV, but also for all kinds of restaurants. There is even a student housing project made of old sea containers. We have a few suggestions for you,if you want to go to 'Noord', but the area is changing so rapidly that we advise you to also visit the following websites: Ilovenoord.nl and Topamsterdam.nl. These websites are also in English.

Film Museum EYE

The ferry

When you leave Amsterdam Central Station at the back you will see several ferries lying at the waterfront. All these ferries are for free. On Ilovenoord.nl you can find a clear overview of all the routes and a timetable (see also the picture on the previous page. Unfortunately this is in Dutch but we think you will understand it). During the day, you will never have to wait long, but sometimes it is useful to know the departure time of the last ferry. The ferries you will probably use most are the Buiksloterweg ferry (to Film Museum EYE) and the NDSM-werf ferry (for example to the IJkantine restaurant).

Film Museum EYE

location 23 IJpromenade, 020 5891400, eyefilm.nl * ferry Buiksloterweg ferry * open museum daily 10 am - 6 pm, restaurant until midnight. The EYEwalk is possible on Wed (noon - 5 pm), Sat + Sun (10 am - 5 pm) * admission film € 10, up to 11 years € 7,50; museum € 9; EYEwalk € 3

This building can simply not be missed and you will certainly see it across the water when waiting for the ferry. EYE was opened in 2012 and has four cinemas, a film lab, changing exhibitions, a restaurant and the largest film library in the Netherlands. In the library they have everything from silent movies from the late 19th century (movies were the actors are not talking) to new movies, but also posters, photos, scenarios and all sorts of other things that have to do with movies. The changing exhibitions are always on a specific theme or part of film history. The exhibitions are not always interesting for children, so check well in advance what they are about. Furthermore EYE organizes outdoor shows, festivals and family shows.

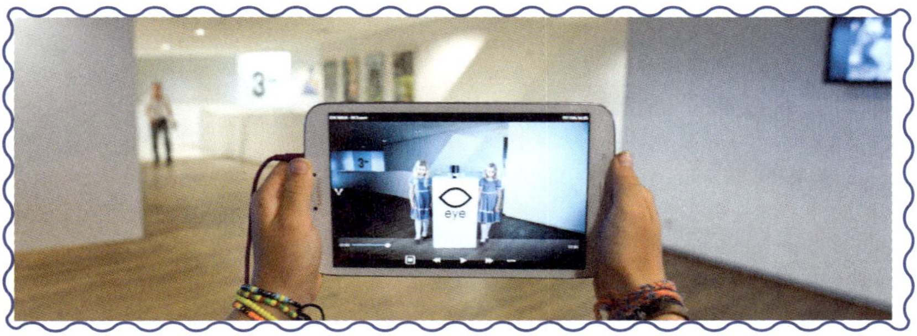

EYEwalk

Children can do the EYEwalk. This is a video tour for children aged 7 to 12 years, during which exciting movies come to life. The EYEwalk takes fifteen minutes and takes you on a video walk through the museum building. You learn how special effects work and you can record a movie scene that you will receive by email. Entrance to the building and the permanent presentation in the basement are for free. Go also to the restaurant, order a drink and in the meantime watch the boats sailing by. Of course you will sit at the waterfront terrace when the weather is nice. And who knows, maybe there is a nice movie playing and your parents let you stay a little longer.

Tolhuistuin

location 5c Buiksloterweg, 020 7630650, tolhuistuin.nl * ferry Buiksloterweg ferry from the rear of Central Station

The Tolhuistuin is right opposite Amsterdam Central Station, across the IJ lake near the Film Museum EYE. It's a nice place to relax and have a drink. At the Tolhuistuin you can eat, chill in the park and enjoy various festivities. To get there take the Buiksloterweg ferry at the rear of Amsterdam Central Station. Within three minutes you will arrive across the water. The entrance of teh Tolhuistuin is a 500-meter walk from the ferry.

IJ-Kantine

location 15-17 MT. Ondinaweg, 020 6337162, ijkantine.nl * ferry NDSM-Werf ferry at the rear of Amsterdam Central Station. It arrives next to the IJ-kantine * open Mon-Sun 9 am - 11 pm

By taking the NDSM-Werf ferry from Amsterdam Central Station you will arrive within ten minutes at the former NDSM shipyard. Here you will find the IJkantine restaurant. This restaurant is located in a building which was once called the Baanderij and which was built by shipbuilders of the NDSM shipyard. At that time (cargo) ships and tankers were built on the grounds, for example for oil company Shell and for the Royal Navy. De Baanderij was used as an assembly hall, as an office and as a canteen. In the 1980s the shipyard went bankrupt and thousands of people lost their jobs. From the IJkantine you have a beautiful view of the waterfront and all the activities on the water. For children there is a play area and in summer there is a huge sandpit. Every Sunday craft afternoons are being organized. The children's menu includes fish fingers with fries, Parma ham with fresh fruits and a delicious pasta.

City Beach and Pllek

location 59 TT Neverittaweg, 020 2900020, Pllek.nl and Noord.amsterdam.nl * ferry NDSM-Werf ferry at the rear of Amsterdam Central Station * open daily 9.30 am - 10 pm

North Amsterdam also has its own city beach and it is located at the NDSM shipyard, right at the IJ lake. With the ferry from Amsterdam Central Station you will get there within a few minutes. From the beach you have a beautiful view over the IJ lake, there's a relaxed atmosphere and for the necessary snacks and drinks go to Pllek. This restaurant is located at the beach. Several fun (children's) activities are being organized like a kids' theatre and craft workshops. On the menu you will find a Monkey Sandwich. Go see for yourself to discover what that is!

Noorderlicht

location 102 NDSM Plein, 020 4922770, noorderlichtcafe.nl * ferry NDSM-Werf ferry or bus 394 or 391 (stop Klaprozenweg), bus 35 (stop Ataturk) * open daily from 11 am

Eating at the Noorderlicht restaurant means that you are at the centre of the former NDSM shipyard, overlooking the IJ lake. The view - especially when the sun goes down - is gorgeous and around Noorderlicht there is plenty of space to romp. The building is also particular because it is a greenhouse made of glass. The food is delicious and sustainable, and all the furnishing is secondhand or found on the street. There is always a good atmosphere and often there is (live) music.

TIP! GO TO THE WEBSITE NDSM.NL (ALSO IN ENGLISH) FOR THE HISTORY OF THIS AREA AND FOR A CALENDAR OF EVENTS.

NDSM Children's Workshop

location 15 TT Neverittaweg, 06 17910832, ndsmkinderatelier.nl * ferry NDSM-Werf ferry or bus 394 or 391 (stop Klaprozenweg), bus 35 (stop Ataturk) * open Sun 2-4 pm, see website for the programme * admission € 10

This workshop is an initiative of artists who work in the shipyard. In a large hangar you can get started on your own artwork, and often there is a special theme. You will work with a variety of residual materials from the artist's workshops, like cardboard, wood, fabric but also old bicycle tires. First you make a design and afterwards you look at the result together. There are four weeks courses but you can also participate in a single lesson.

IJscuypje

location 30 MS. van Riemsdijkweg, ijscuypje.nl * ferry NDSM-Werf ferry and continue on foot

The first branch of this ice cream shop is located on the Albert Cuyp market, hence the name 'Cuypje'. IJscuypje has currently eleven shops in Amsterdam, one of which is at the NDSM shipyard. All the ice cream is made with natural ingredients and you can choose from eighteen flavors of sorbet, ice cream or frozen yogurt. The flavors change regulary and do you have food allergies? On the website of IJscuypje you can see exactly what flavors you are allowed to eat and what flavors you better don't eat.

The Animal Island

location 11 Molenwijk 11, 020 4920464, hetdiereneiland.nl * bus 35 (stop Pomonastraat) * open Mon + Fri noon - 5 pm, Tue-Thu 10 am - 5 pm, Sat noon - 5 pm. Apr-Oct also on Sun (noon - 5 pm) * admission free

The Animal Island (Diereneiland in Dutch) in Molenwijk is a petting zoo and playground. In early 2012 it was all renovated and the results are impressive. You can play, build huts and assist in taking care of the animals. There is a large rabbit warren, there are turkeys, peacocks, sheep, goats and much more. You can also buy freshly laid eggs.

The Vliegenbos

location vliegenbos.info * bus 32 or 33 (stop Merelstraat)

The Vliegenbos forrest is located in North Amsterdam, and is officially called the WH Vliegenbos. It is the oldest city forest of Amsterdam and is over 100 years old. This forest is as a forest should be. For the most part nature is allowed to grow without human intervention, so there are not so many neatly raked paths. Especially the many elm trees make this forest unique. And the number of elm trees is quite astonishing considering the fact that most of the trees were cut down during World War II. The wood was then used as firewood by the inhabitants of Amsterdam. But one avenue of elms and around a hundred trees survived the war. After the war the felled trees began to grow again and now this forest is famous for its large amount of elms. As you can imagine, you can enjoy cycling and hiking in the forrest and there is also a children's playground. Currently a Walkway throught the Wild and a natural playgrond are being constructed. Do you fancy a walk in the woods? Notice that the entrances to the park are not clearly indicated. The most obvious entrance can be found at the Meeuwenlaan.

TIP! YOU CAN ALSO GO CAMPING IN THE WOODS OR SLEEP IN THE CAMP HOTEL (SEE PAGE 16).

CAN YOU IDENTIFY AN ELM TREE? THE EASIEST WAY IS TO LOOK AT THE LEAF OF AN ELM. ELM LEAVES ALTERNATE ALONG 2 SIDES OF THE STEM. THE LEAF IS OVAL IN SHAPE AND COMES TO A POINT AT THE END. THE EDGES OF THE LEAF ARE JAGGED AND THE VEINS ARE PROMINENT. TAKE A LOOK AT THE PICTURE ON THE NEXT PAGE AND TRY TO FIND THE ELMS!

NOORDERPARKBAD

location **5 Sneeuwbalweg, noord.amsterdam.nl** * **bus** **391 (stop Pinksterbloemstraat), 35 (stop Sneeuwbalstraat)** * **open and amission** **opening hours and admission prices were not yet known at the time of the compilation of this guide**

In early 2015 the Noorderparkbad swimming pool will open its doors. It will be a sustainable and energy efficient pool with a sunbathing area and outside and inside pool. The Noorderparkbad will replace the Floraparkbad, which is now obsolete.

TIP: DO YOU WANT TO STAY THE NIGHT IN A HARBOUR? MAYBE YOUR PARENTS CAN BOOK A ROOM AT THE BOTEL AND YOU CAN SLEEP ON A LARGE SHIP. SEE AMSTELBOTEL.NL FOR MORE INFORMATION.

184. Ulmus campestris L.

Feldrüster.

EAST AMSTERDAM

The East of Amsterdam is the large area stretching from the Waterlooplein near the centre to the Bijlmer, a neighbourhood known for the Amsterdam ArenA football stadium. There are several interesting museums in East Amsterdam, but it also has the oldest zoo in the Netherlands: Artis. We love this part of the city, mainly because it is not so crowded with tourists. It is a residential area and most buildings consist of appartments instead of offices.

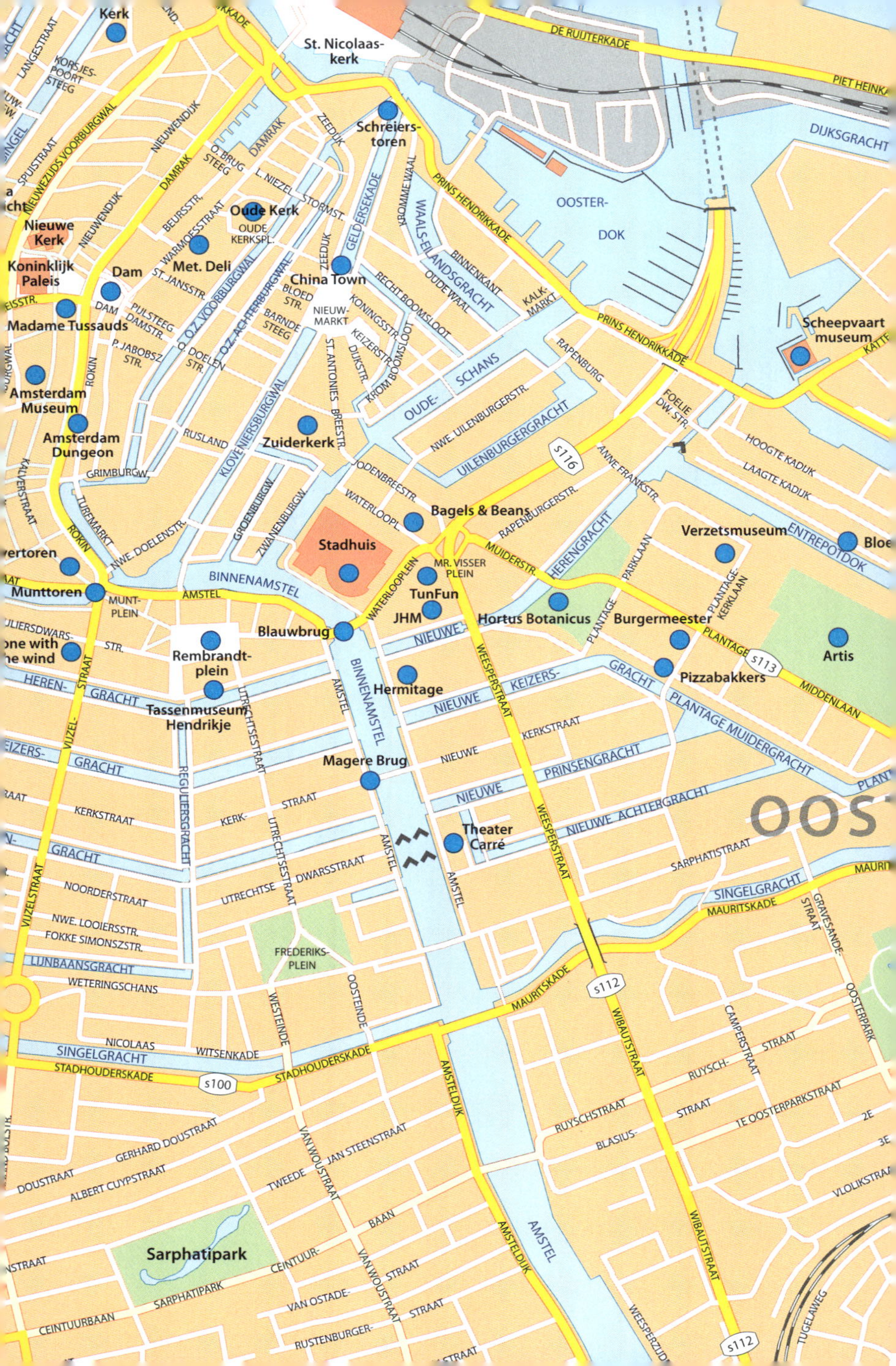

Kerk
St. Nicolaas-
kerk
DE RUIJTERKADE
PIET HEINKA
DIJKSGRACHT
LANGESTRAAT
KORSJES-
POORT
STEEG
SINGEL
SPUISTRAAT
NIEUWEZIJDS VOORBURGWAL
NIEUWENDIJK
DAMRAK
O. BRUG
STEEG
L. NIEZEL
ZEEDIJK
Schreiers-
toren
KROMME WAAL
GELDERSEKADE
WAALS-EILANDSGRACHT
PRINS HENDRIKKADE
OOSTER-
DOK
Oude Kerk
OUDE
KERKSPL.
STORMST.
Nieuwe
Kerk
Koninklijk
Paleis
Met. Deli
WARMOESSTRAAT
BEURSSTR.
China Town
ZEEDIJK
RECHT BOOMSSLOOT
BINNENKANT
OUDE WAAL
KALK-
MARKT
Dam
DAM
ST. JANSSTR.
PIJLSTEEG
DAMSTR.
Madame Tussauds
BLOED
STR.
BARNDE
STEEG
NIEUW-
MARKT
KONINGSSTR.
KEIZERSSTR.
DIJKSTR.
KROM BOOMSLOOT
Scheepvaart
museum
KATTE
RAPENBURG
P. JABOBSZ
STR.
O.Z. VOORBURGWAL
O.Z. ACHTERBURGWAL
DOELEN
STR.
ROKIN
Amsterdam
Museum
OUDE-
SCHANS
NWE. UILENBURGERSTR.
UILENBURGERGRACHT
FOELIE
DW. STR.
HOOGTE KADIJK
LAAGTE KADIJK
Amsterdam
Dungeon
RUSLAND
KLOVENIERSBURGWAL
Zuiderkerk
ST. ANTONIES BREESTR.
s116
ANNE FRANKSTR.
GRIMBURGW.
KALVERSTRAAT
JODENBREESTR.
WATERLOOPL.
Bagels & Beans
RAPENBURGERSTR.
Verzetsmuseum
ENTREPOTDOK
Bloe
GROENBURGW.
ZWANENBURGW.
TURFMARKT
NWE. DOELENSTR.
Stadhuis
MR. VISSER
PLEIN
MUIDERSTR.
HERENGRACHT
PARKLAAN
PLANTAGE-
KERKLAAN
Munttoren
MUNT-
PLEIN
AMSTEL
BINNENAMSTEL
TunFun
WATERLOOPLEIN
JHM
Hortus Botanicus
PLANTAGE
Burgermeester
Blauwbrug
NIEUWE
Rembrandt-
plein
STR.
HEREN-
GRACHT
VIJZEL-
STRAAT
PLANTAGE
s113
MIDDENLAAN
Artis
Pizzabakkers
Hermitage
KEIZERS-
GRACHT
PLANTAGE MUIDERGRACHT
Tassenmuseum
Hendrikje
UTRECHTSESTRAAT
WEESPERSTRAAT
KERKSTRAAT
KEIZERS-
GRACHT
REGULIERSGRACHT
Magere Brug
NIEUWE
PRINSENGRACHT
NIEUWE
KERKSTRAAT
KERK-
STRAAT
NIEUWE ACHTERGRACHT
OOST
Theater
Carré
GRACHT
UTRECHTSE
DWARSSTRAAT
SARPHATISTRAAT
MAURI
SINGELGRACHT
MAURITSKADE
NOORDERSTRAAT
NWE. LOOIERSSTR.
FOKKE SIMONSZSTR.
FREDERIKS-
PLEIN
GRAVESANDE-
STRAAT
LIJNBAANSGRACHT
WETERINGSCHANS
s112
WESTEINDE
OOSTEINDE
CAMPERSTRAAT
OOSTERPARK
NICOLAAS
WITSENKADE
SINGELGRACHT
STADHOUDERSKADE
s100
AMSTELDIJK
WIBAUTSTRAAT
RUYSCH-
STRAAT
RUYSCHSTRAAT
BLASIUS-
1E OOSTERPARKSTRAAT
2E
3E
GERHARD DOUSTRAAT
DOUSTRAAT
ALBERT CUYPSTRAAT
TWEEDE
JAN STEENSTRAAT
VAN WOUSTRAAT
VLOLIKSTRA
BAAN
Sarphatipark
CEINTUUR-
SARPHATIPARK
CEINTUURBAAN
VAN OSTADE-
RUSTENBURGER-
WEESPERZIJDE
TUGELAWEG

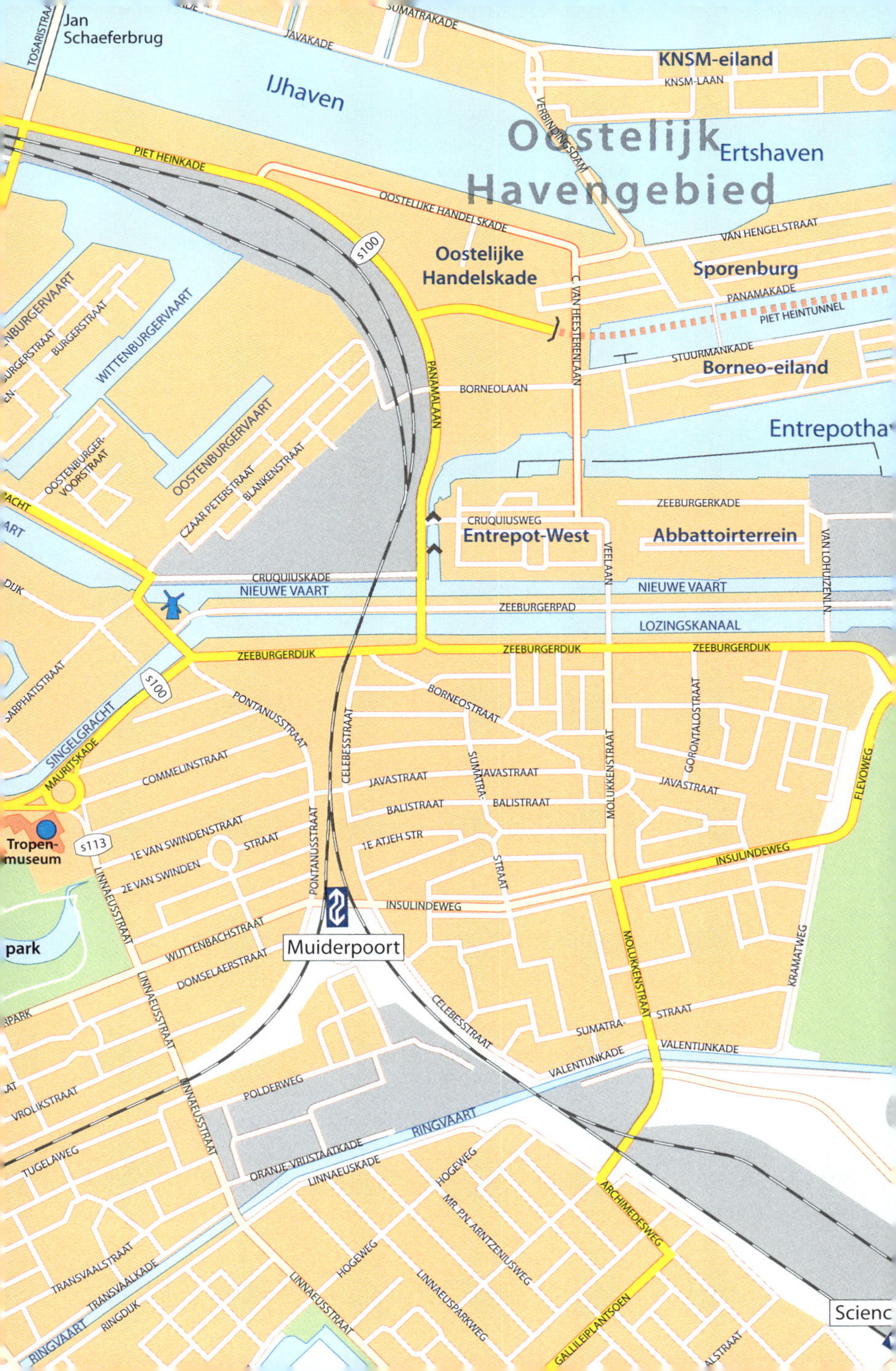

Jan Schaeferbrug
TOSARISTRAAT
JAVAKADE
SUMATRAKADE
KNSM-eiland
KNSM-LAAN
IJhaven
Oostelijk Havengebied
Ertshaven
VERBINDINGSDAM
PIET HEINKADE
OOSTELIJKE HANDELSKADE
VAN HENGELSTRAAT
s100
Oostelijke Handelskade
Sporenburg
PANAMAKADE
PIET HEINTUNNEL
C. VAN EESTERENLAAN
STUURMANKADE
Borneo-eiland
WITTENBURGERVAART
BURGERSTRAAT
PANAMALAAN
BORNEOLAAN
Entrepotha
OOSTENBURGERVAART
OOSTENBURGER-VOORSTRAAT
CZAAR PETERSTRAAT
BLANKENSTRAAT
ZEEBURGERKADE
CRUQUIUSWEG
Entrepot-West
Abbattoirterrein
VEELAAN
VAN LOHUIZENLN
CRUQUIUSKADE
NIEUWE VAART
ZEEBURGERPAD
LOZINGSKANAAL
ZEEBURGERDIJK
SARPHATISTRAAT
SINGELGRACHT
MAURITSKADE
PONTANUSSTRAAT
BORNEOSTRAAT
CELEBESSTRAAT
GORONTALOSTRAAT
MOLUKKENSTRAAT
FLEVOWEG
COMMELINSTRAAT
JAVASTRAAT
SUMATRA-
BALISTRAAT
1E ATJEH STR
Tropen-museum
s113
1E VAN SWINDENSTRAAT
2E VAN SWINDEN
STRAAT
INSULINDEWEG
LINNAEUSSTRAAT
park
Muiderpoort
WIJTTENBACHSTRAAT
DOMSELAERSTRAAT
KRAMATWEG
SUMATRA-
STRAAT
VALENTIJNKADE
VROLIKSTRAAT
POLDERWEG
RINGVAART
TUGELAWEG
ORANJE-VRIJSTAATKADE
LINNAEUSKADE
HOGEWEG
MR. P.N. ARNTZENIUSWEG
ARCHIMEDESWEG
TRANSVAALSTRAAT
TRANSVAALKADE
RINGDIJK
LINNAEUSPARKWEG
GALILEIPLANTSOEN
Scienc

WATERLOOPLEIN

location waterloopleinmarkt.nl * tram 9 and 14 (stop Waterlooplein), metro 51, 53 and 54 (stop Waterlooplein) * open Mon-Sat 9 am - 5 pm

Amsterdam's largest flea market is located on the Waterlooplein, the square near city hall. The market dates back to 1893 and you can spend a lot of time browsing the stalls. Of course there are no actual fleas on offer, but all kinds of second-hand goods. Old prom dresses and shoes for example, but also furniture, vintage jeans and leather jackets.

BAGELS AND BEANS

location 2 Waterlooplein, 020 4288906, bagelsbeans.nl * tram 9 and 14 (stop Waterlooplein), metro 51, 53 and 54 (stop Waterlooplein) * open Mon-Sat 8.31 am - 5.32 pm, Sun 10.58 am - 5.31 pm

And while you are browsing the stalls on the Waterlooplein, don't forget to visit Bagels & Beans for a delicious fresh bagel. From behind the circular windows you will have a perfect view of the visitors of the market or find yourself a good spot on the terrace. Enjoy your bagel like the Dutch do, with chocolate sprinkles ('hagelslag') or with banana and cinnamon.

DO YOU KNOW WHAT A BAGEL IS? A BAGEL IS A CIRCULAR AND SEMI-HARD ROLL WITH A HOLE IN THE MIDDLE. AN AUSTRIAN BAKER INVENTED THIS SANDWICH IN THE 16TH CENTURY TO THANK THE KING OF POLAND. LATER - WHEN MANY PEOPLE FROM EASTERN EUROPE IMMIGRATED TO THE UNITED STATES - THE BAGEL BECAME VERY POPULAR IN JEWISH NEIGHBOURHOODS IN THE BIG CITIES.

TUNFUN

location **7 Mr. Visserplein, 020 6894300, tunfun.nl** * **tram** **9 and 14 (stop Mr. Visserplein),** **metro** **51, 53 and 54 (stop Waterlooplein)** * **open** **daily 10 am - 6 pm** * **admission** **1-18 years € 8,50; adults and babies free**

Did you ever play in an old car tunnel? No? Take your chance at TunFun underneath the Mr. Visserplein. This huge indoor playground (4,000 m2!) is a paradise for children from ages 0 to 12. Babies and infants can play with soft toys and soft slides, whereas older kids have fun on the trampolines, the slides and the jungle gym. For parents there is free Wi-Fi, a large seating and lounge area, a reading table and they can even get earplugs if the noise of screaming children gets too loud for them. Go to HapSap for a drink and healthy snack and tell your mother of the special children's toilets, high chairs, the microwave to heat bottles and the changing room. On the website (also in English) you can see if and when fun activities are being organized at TunFun, which is often the case.

Hermitage Amsterdam

location 51 Amstel, 020 5308755, hermitage.nl * tram 9 and 14 (stop Waterlooplein), metro 51, 53 and 54 (stop Waterlooplein – exit Nieuwe Herengracht) * open daily 10 am - 5 pm * admission prices vary depending on the exhibition, around € 15, 6-16 years € 5

Since 2009 the Hermitage Amsterdam has become one of the most popular museums in Amsterdam. The impressive building in which the museum is currently housed was for 324 years a home for the elderly. Hermitage Amsterdam is part of the famous Hermitage in St. Petersburg in Russia, one of the largest art museums in the world. The exhibitions change every six months; take a look at the website for information on the current and upcoming exhibitions.

Hermitage for children

At the Hermitage Amsterdam children get special attention. There is a separate building for the Hermitage for Children, the Neerlandia building, with some nice workshops, classrooms, a children's canteen and children's gift shop. The programmes are mainly for children from primary schools in the Amsterdam region. Every first Sunday of the month, you can get an interactive tour of the exhibition in the 'regular' Hermitage, under the guidance of a professional teacher. Unfortunately this tour is in Dutch, but we are pretty sure you can ask the tour guide to translate some information for you. Afterwards you can participate in one of the creative workshops (a reservation is required).

Hortus Botanicus

location 2a Plantage Middenlaan, 020 6259021, dehortus.nl * tram 9 and 14 (stop Mr. Visserplein), metro 51, 53 and 54 (stop Waterlooplein – exit Hortusplantsoen) * open daily 10 am - 5 pm * admission € 8,50, 5-14 years € 4,50

The Hortus Botanicus Amsterdam is one of the oldest botanical gardens in the world. A botanical garden is a scientific garden where plants grow and flourish for people to study them. In the Hortus you will find around 6,000 plants of over 4,000 different species. They all have a Dutch name and a scientific name. When the Hortus Botanicus was laid out (in the 17th century) leaves and flowers from the garden were used for the preparation of medicines. The trees and plants that are currently growing in the garden originate from all parts of the world. The history of the Victoria water lily for example, has its beginnings in South America. Since 1859 the giant lily has flowered regularly in the Amsterdam Hortus and when this happens people stand in line for hours to see it. The leaves of the flower can reach a diameter of 3 metres and they are so strong that they can support a weight of 40 kilos. The flower opens only for two nights.

Royal plant

The Eastern Cape giant cycad came to the Netherlands around 300 years ago and the Hortus bought it in 1850 from King William II. The plants of this species are either male or female. The tree in the Hortus is a male plant. The scientific name is *Encephalartos altensteinii* and the first part of the name is Greek for 'bread in the centre'. In ancient Greece people used the centre of the stem as food. Do you want to discover some more special plants? At the entrance you can collect the free Superplants map (in English!) featuring 15 record keepers in the world of plants. The map can also be downloaded from the children's website **Dehortuskids.nl.** When you get thirsty or hungry, take a seat at the Orangery and order a delicious juice and piece of cake. On the terrace you are surrounded by all kinds of exotic plants, making this one of the most beautiful outdoor cafés in Amsterdam.

THE HORTUS BOTANICUS AMSTERDAM HOUSES ABOUT 1% OF ALL PLANT SPECIES GROWING ON EARTH. ON THE WEBSITE YOU CAN FIND A DATABASE FEATURING THE PLANTS AND THEIR LOCATION IN THE GARDEN.

ARTIS

location 38-40 Plantage Kerklaan, 0900 2784796, artis.nl * tram 9 and 14 (stop Artis), metro 51, 53 and 54 (stop Waterlooplein - exit Hortus) * open Nov-Feb 9 am - 5 pm, Mar-Oct 9 am - 6 pm, Jun, Jul, Aug every Sat until sundown * admission € 19,95, 3-9 years € 16,50

Artis opened its doors in 1838 and it is the oldest zoo in the Netherlands. Until 1851 access to Artis was granted only to a select group of members, not to the ordinary people

Ronald van Weeren

of Amsterdam. Nowadays, the zoo houses more than 900 species of animals, varying from wildebeest to butterflies, from tropical fish to tigers and giraffes. In recent years there have been extensive renovations to give animals, plants and visitors more space. Artis' highlights include the huge aquarium, the African savannah, the butterfly garden and the big climbing complex for kids near the gazelles. At this spot you can also find an enormous restaurant to take a break. Be sure to visit the Planetarium, with daily screenings in the large spherical dome. Travel through the solar system, visit the deep sea and accompany Darwin to the Galapagos Islands. Do your parents need a stroller? They can loan them at several spots in the zoo (for a deposit of 2 euros). It is nice to take a look on the website before you visit the zoo in order to know the feeding programme of the day. Print it, so you are on time for the feeding of the vultures or the training of the sea lions.

Summernights at the Zoo

Fun: in June, July and August you can visit Artis on Saturdays until sundown. Artists perform on several locations in the zoo and food and drinks for a picknick are for sale.

Tip!

Ask your parents to download the free Artis app featuring several fun theme routes, for example a route along ten 'forgotten animals'. The app also contains a map, information about zookeeper talks en fun facts. Also convenient: the daily calendar with feeding times and the latest news.

DO YOU NOT WANT TO TRAVEL TO THE ZOO BY METRO OR TRAM? THEN TAKE THE ARTIS ROYAL ZOO EXPRESS FROM BOAT COMPANY LOVERS (OPPOSITE AMSTERDAM CENTRAL STATION). THIS BOAT TAKES YOU IN 20 MINUTES TO THE ZOO AND AFTERWARDS YOU GET A NICE CRUISE THROUGH THE CANALS OF THE CITY. VISIT LOVERS.NL FOR MORE INFORMATION.

Bloem 36

location 36 Entrepotdok, 020 3300929, bloem36.nl * tram 9 and 14 (stop Artis), metro 51, 53 and 54 (stop Waterlooplein - exit Hortus) * open daily 11 am-12 pm

This restaurant is located in an old warehouse situated near the entrance of the zoo. It has a very nice terrace, and equally nice food. There is no special children's menu, but there are many sandwiches to choose from, including a delicious 'wentelteefje'. A wentelteefje consists of bread that is first dipped in milk and then fried in butter and sprinkled with sugar.

De Pizzabakkers

location 2 Plantage Kerklaan, 020 6250740, depizzabakkers.nl; also at 16 1e Sweelinckstraat, 128 Haarlemmerdijk, 501 Overtoom * tram 9 and 14 (stop Artis), metro 51, 53 and 54 (stop Waterlooplein - exit Hortus) * open Mon-Thu 12 am-10 pm, Fri 12 am-11 pm, Sat 4 pm-11 pm, Sun 4 pm-10 pm

De Pizzabakkers uses ingredients from small artisan producers for its pizza, like sausages from a family business in Tuscany. There are four Pizzabakkers restaurants in Amsterdam, including this one near Artis. At De Pizzabakkers you can order pizza, as well as all kinds of pasta, salads and antipasti. And don't forget the ice cream or dolci! Also on the menu: play dough. Not for eating, but for creating your own dough characters.

Dutch Resistance Museum

location Plantage Kerklaan 61, 020 6202535, verzetsmuseum.org * tram 9 and 14 (stop Plantage Kerklaan, Plantage Middenlaan/Kerklaan or Artis), metro 51, 53 and 54 (stop Waterlooplein - exit Hortus) * open Tue-Fri 10 am - 5 pm, Sat-Mon 11 am - 5 pm * admission € 10, 7-15 years € 5

The children's section of the Dutch Resistance Museum (Verzetsmuseum) – opposite the entrance of Artis – opened its doors at the end of 2013. This part of the museum is aimed at children from the age of nine and the texts and audio are available in both Dutch and English. Take a time machine and travel to the Netherlands during World War II. Explore the (true) stories of four children: Eva, Jan, Nelly and Henk. You will learn about their lives during the German occupation (did they go to school for example?) and you will discover what they went through and which difficult choices they had to make. On the website of the museum you can already meet the four children of the exhibition. Children from the age of fourteen can visit the museum with a free audio tour (also available in English).

THE SURROUNDINGS OF THE DUTCH RESISTANCE MUSEUM ARE CLOSELY CONNECTED WITH THE HISTORY OF THE OCCUPATION AND THE RESISTANCE MOVEMENT. ON THE WEBSITE OF THE DUTCH RESISTANCE MUSEUM YOU CAN DOWNLOAD WALKS THROUGH THE NEIGHBOURHOOD OF THE MUSEUM. THESE WALKS ARE DEDICATED TO WORLD WAR TWO. YOU LEARN FOR EXAMPLE WHY THE GERMANS LOVED THE ARTIS ZOO. IN THE ZOO PEOPLE COULD SEE WITH THEIR OWN EYES THAT ONLY THE STRONGEST ANIMALS AND BREEDS SURVIVED. THE SHORT WALK TAKES ABOUT 25 MINUTES, THE LONGER WALK 45 MINUTES.

© Ivar Pel

Tropenmuseum Junior

location 2 Linnaeusstraat, 020 5688300, tropenmuseumjunior.nl * bus 22 (stop Oostenburgergracht), tram 3, 7 and 10 (stop Linnaeusstraat), 9 (stop 1e van Swindenstraat) * open Tropenmuseum Tue-Sun 10 am - 5 pm, Tropenmuseum Junior weekends + holidays, visit the website for the current programme and timetable * admission € 12,50, 4-17 years € 8

The Tropenmuseum Junior was founded in 1975 as a part of the 'regular' Tropenmuseum (Amsterdam Tropical Museum). It was the first children's museum in Europe. In 2012 the Tropenmuseum Junior won the Children's Museum Award, a price for the best children's museum in the world. We completely understand the jury's choice, because every weekend the Tropenmuseum Junior organizes all kinds of creative activities for different ages and there are always fun, interactive exhibitions. The exhibition changes every three years. While writing this guide, it was MixMax Brazil, focused on the diverse culture of Brazil. If you visit MixMax Brazil you get to wear flipflops, you will walk the wobbly boards between the mangrove roots and end up on a Brazilian town square surrounded by dozens of doors, a bottle cave and a roof terrace with sea view.

Family visits

The Tropenmuseum Junior is intended for children aged 6 to 13 years and their families. Visiting families can choose between a 90-minute programme for children or a guided tour of the exhibition where children and parents stay together. Most programmes are in Dutch, but English programmes are available on request. During the 30-minute guided tour the museum staff will guide you through the exhibition. The tours start every 30 minutes. Would you like to learn more about the culture featured in the exhibition? Check the website for interesting background information, music and videos.

© Ivar Pel

Burgermeester

location **37 Plantage Kerklaan, 0900 2874377, burgermeester.eu. Also restaurants at 130 Elandsgracht and 48 Albert Cuypstraat** * **tram** **9 and 14 (stop Artis),** **metro** **51, 53 and 54 (stop Waterlooplein - exit Hortus)** * **open** **daily 12 am - 11 pm**

For the best burgers in Amsterdam go to one of the three restaurants of Burgermeester (Dutch for 'mayor'). All the food is 'fair', which means that everything on your plate is fresh and produced with the environment in mind. Many products are bought in the region and even the mayonnaise is homemade. Every burger can be ordered in a small version and there are also veggie burgers on the menu. Do you have a good idea for a burger? Let the cook at Burgermeester know through the website and maybe your idea will be the new Burger of the Month. And are you wondering where the cutlery is? You are allowed to eat with your hands!

Children's Jewish Historical Museum

location 1 Nieuwe Amstelstraat, 020 5310310, jhmkindermuseum.nl * metro 51, 53 and 54 (stop Waterlooplein - exit Nieuwe Amstelstraat), tram 9 and 14 (stop Waterlooplein) * open daily 11 am - 5 pm * admission € 12, 13-17 years € 6, 6-12 years € 3; the ticket can also be used for the Portugese synagogue, the Jewish Historical Museum and the Hollandsche Schouwburg

The Children's Jewish Historical Museum (Joods Historisch Museum Kinderen) is located in the old Jewish quarter of Amsterdam and is part of the Jewish Historical Museum. You will visit the three-storey house of the Jewish Hollander family. Max the Matzo gives you a tour of their home. In each room you learn something about Jewish traditions and customs. In the kitchen for example, you will discover what kosher food is and in the study you will find the Torah, the Jewish holy book. On the entertaining website of the Children's Jewish Historical Museum you can already take a look at the virtual house, listen to Jewish music, send E-cards and even create your own room.

LOOK CLOSELY AT THE BUILDING OF THE MUSEUM. IT IS AN ANCIENT SYNAGOGUE AND THIS IS A JEWISH HOUSE OF PRAYER.

Amsterdam Arena

location **1 ArenA Boulevard, Entrance E (starting point), 020 3111336, amsterdamarena.nl** * **metro** **54 (stop Bijlmer ArenA)** * **open** **Kidstour: Wen, Sat and Sun afternoon + during school holidays; Stadion tour daily 5x** * **admission** **Kids Tour € 13 (5-12 years), Stadium Tour € 14,50, 5-12 years € 9,50**

Football fans will definitely want to visit the Amsterdam ArenA, the stadium of the famous Dutch football team Ajax. Unfortunately the World of Ajax Kids Tour for children aged 5 to 12 is only in Dutch, but English spoken tours are available on request. The regular Stadium Tour is available in Dutch and English. You will stand along the lines, touch the leather business seats next to the dug-out and you will visit the press stand. If Ajax is not training or playing, you can even visit the dressing room area. Sometimes you can see the players training. Check the Ajax website (Ajax.nl) for the training schedule.

AJAX IS THE MOST SUCCESFUL FOOTBALL CLUB IN THE NETHERLANDS. MAYBE YOU HAVE HEARD ABOUT ONE OF THE MOST FAMOUS FOOTBALL PLAYERS OF ALL TIMES: JOHAN CRUIJFF. HE PLAYED AT AJAX BETWEEN 1959-1973 AND 1981-1983. WITH THE TEAM HE WON THREE EUROPEAN CUPS. HE WORE THE SHIRT WITH NUMBER 14 AND WHEN HE RETIRED THE SHIRT RETIRED WITH HIM. NO OTHER AJAX PLAYER WILL WEAR THAT NUMBER EVER AGAIN.

SOUTH AMSTERDAM

The most famous Amsterdam museums are located in the south of the city: the Van Gogh Museum, the Rijksmuseum and the Stedelijk Museum. But this neighbourhood is also famous for its parks and gardens. The Vondelpark for example is a real hot spot, but the Amsterdamse Bos and the Amstelpark are also worth a visit. Enjoy!

Sunflowers by Vincent Van Gogh

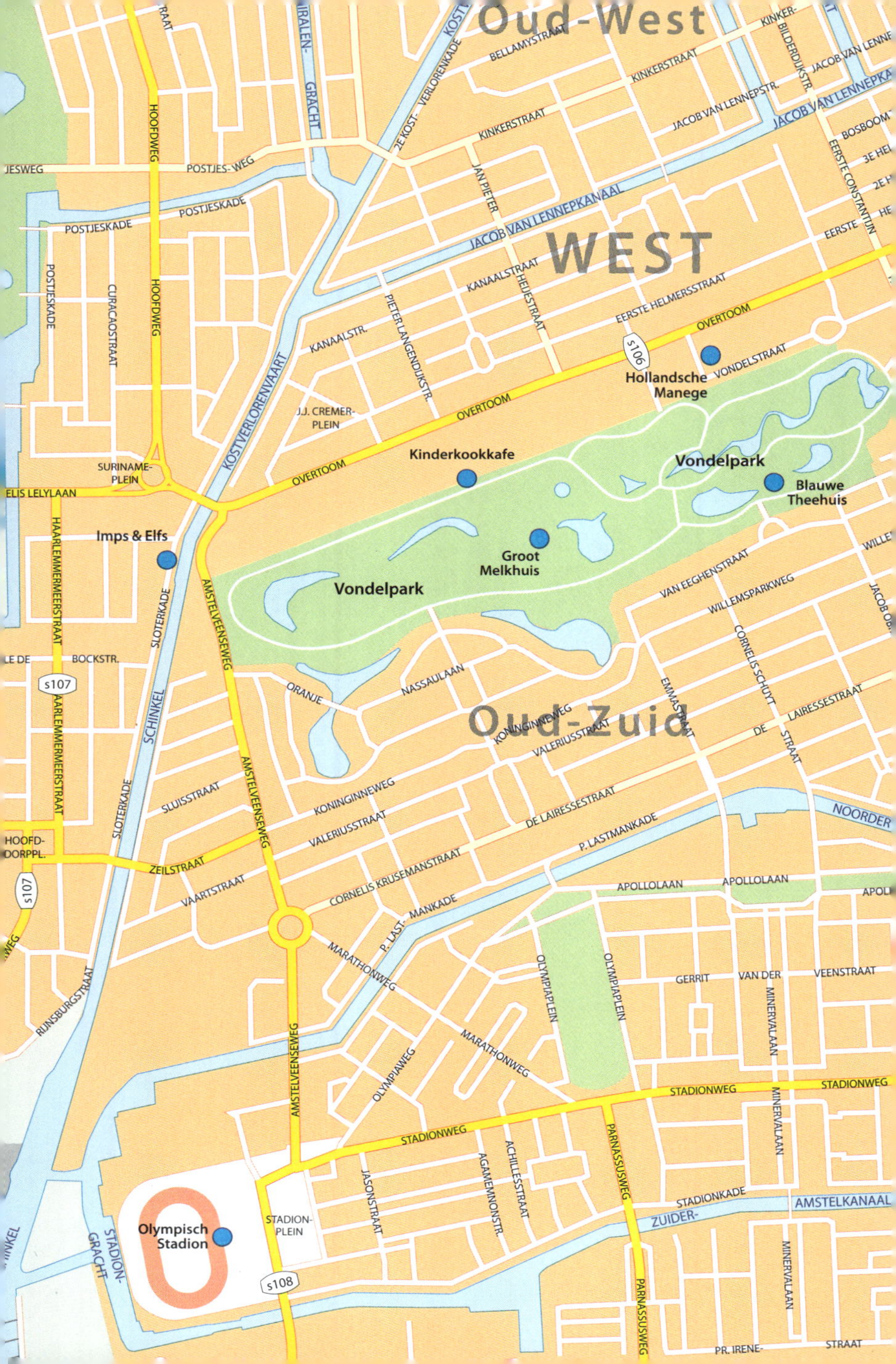

Oud-West
WEST
Oud-Zuid
Vondelpark
Vondelpark
Hollandsche Manege
Kinderkookkafe
Blauwe Theehuis
Groot Melkhuis
Imps & Elfs
Olympisch Stadion
OVERTOOM
VONDELSTRAAT
KINKERSTRAAT
BELLAMYSTRAAT
JACOB VAN LENNEPKANAAL
JACOB VAN LENNEPSTR.
EERSTE HELMERSSTRAAT
KANAALSTRAAT
KANAALSTR.
HEEJESTRAAT
JAN PIETER
PIETER LANGENDIJKSTR.
J.J. CREMER-PLEIN
KOSTVERLORENVAART
2E KOST- VERLORENKADE
BILDERDIJKSTR.
EERSTE CONSTANTIJN
BOSBOOM
POSTJES-WEG
POSTJESKADE
CURACAOSTRAAT
HOOFDWEG
SURINAME-PLEIN
ELIS LELYLAAN
HAARLEMMERMEERSTRAAT
BOCKSTR.
SLOTERKADE
SCHINKEL
AMSTELVEENSEWEG
s106
s107
s108
ORANJE
NASSAULAAN
KONINGINNEWEG
VALERIUSSTRAAT
VAN EEGHENSTRAAT
WILLEMSPARKWEG
CORNELIS SCHUYT STRAAT
EMMASTRAAT
DE LAIRESSESTRAAT
NOORDER
P. LASTMANKADE
APOLLOLAAN
SLUISSTRAAT
ZEILSTRAAT
HOOFD-DORPPL.
VAARTSTRAAT
CORNELIS KRUSEMANSTRAAT
P. LAST- MANKADE
MARATHONWEG
OLYMPIAPLEIN
OLYMPIAWEG
GERRIT VAN DER VEENSTRAAT
MINERVALAAN
STADIONWEG
RIJNSBURGSTRAAT
STADION-PLEIN
STADION-GRACHT
JASONSTRAAT
AGAMEMNONSTR.
ACHILLESSTRAAT
PARNASSUSWEG
STADIONKADE
ZUIDER- AMSTELKANAAL
PR. IRENE- STRAAT

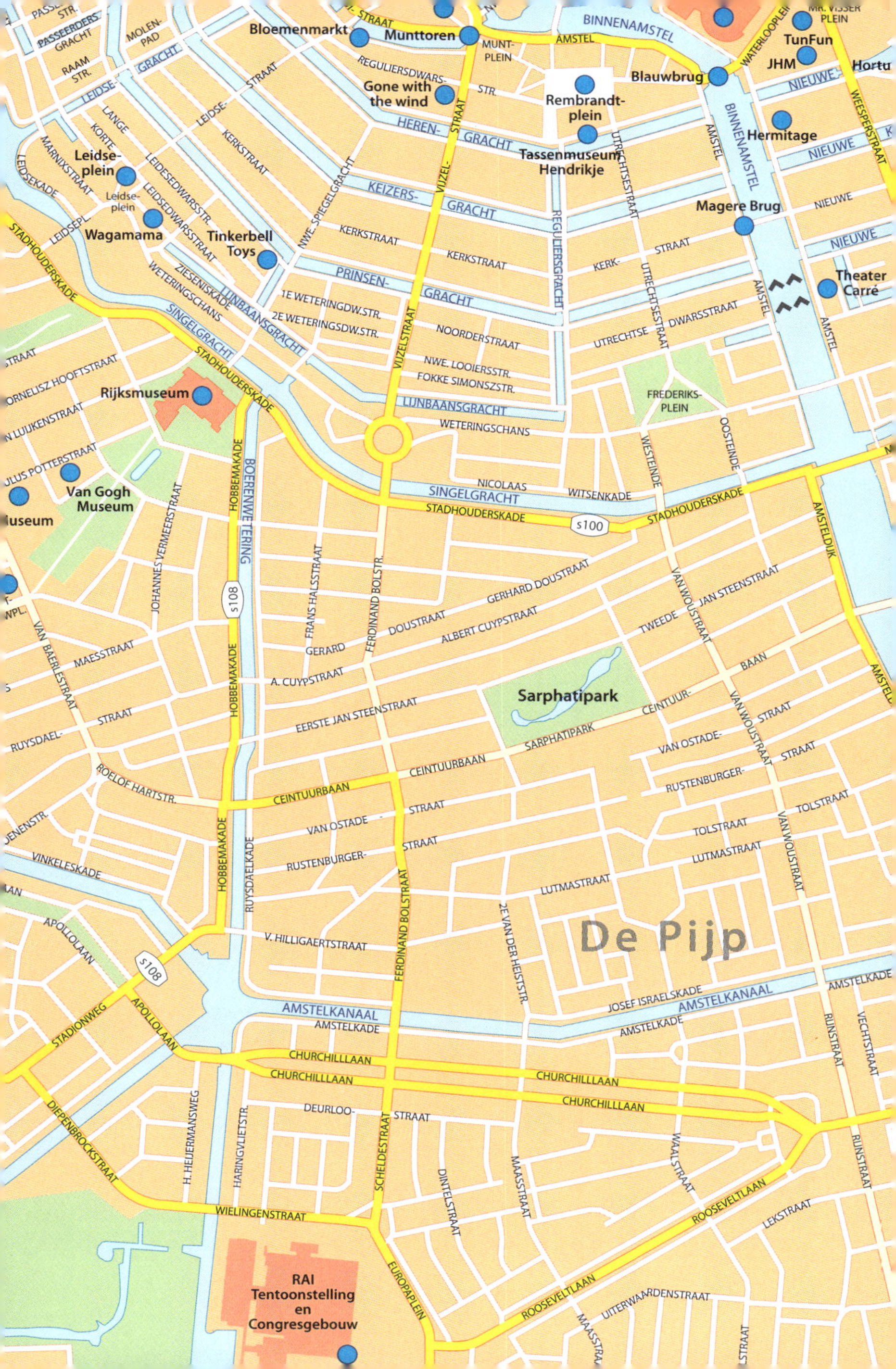

Bloemenmarkt
Munttoren
MUNT-PLEIN
BINNENAMSTEL
AMSTEL
WATERLOOPLEIN
MR. VISSER PLEIN
TunFun
JHM
Hortu
Blauwbrug
Gone with the wind
REGULIERSDWARS-STR.
Rembrandt-plein
Tassenmuseum Hendrikje
Hermitage
HEREN-GRACHT
KEIZERS-GRACHT
PRINSEN-GRACHT
VIJZELSTRAAT
UTRECHTSESTRAAT
REGULIERSGRACHT
Magere Brug
Theater Carré
NIEUWE
WEESPERSTRAAT
PASSEERDERS GRACHT
MOLEN-PAD
RAAM STR.
LEIDSE-GRACHT
LEIDSESTRAAT
LEIDSEKADE
MARNIXSTRAAT
KORTE LANGE LEIDSEDWARSSTR.
Leidse-plein
Wagamama
Tinkerbell Toys
KERKSTRAAT
NWE. SPIEGELGRACHT
LIJNBAANSGRACHT
ZIESENISKADE
WETERINGSCHANS
SINGELGRACHT
STADHOUDERSKADE
1E WETERINGDW.STR.
2E WETERINGSDW.STR.
NOORDERSTRAAT
NWE. LOOIERSSTR.
FOKKE SIMONSZSTR.
UTRECHTSE DWARSSTRAAT
FREDERIKS-PLEIN
WESTEINDE
OOSTEINDE
Rijksmuseum
CORNELISZ HOOFTSTRAAT
VAN LUIJKENSTRAAT
PAULUS POTTERSTRAAT
Van Gogh Museum
HOBBEMAKADE
BOERENWETERING
JOHANNES VERMEERSTRAAT
NICOLAAS WITSENKADE
s100
s108
AMSTELDIJK
VAN BAERLESTRAAT
MAESSTRAAT
RUYSDAELSTRAAT
ROELOF HARTSTR.
FRANS HALSSTRAAT
FERDINAND BOLSTR.
GERARD DOUSTRAAT
GERHARD DOUSTRAAT
ALBERT CUYPSTRAAT
A. CUYPSTRAAT
EERSTE JAN STEENSTRAAT
JAN STEENSTRAAT
TWEEDE JAN STEENSTRAAT
VAN WOUSTRAAT
Sarphatipark
SARPHATIPARK
CEINTUURBAAN
VAN OSTADE-STRAAT
RUSTENBURGER-STRAAT
TOLSTRAAT
LUTMASTRAAT
VINKELESKADE
RUYSDAELKADE
FERDINAND BOLSTRAAT
2E VAN DER HELSTSTR.
De Pijp
APOLLOLAAN
V. HILLIGAERTSTRAAT
STADIONWEG
JOSEF ISRAELSKADE
AMSTELKANAAL
AMSTELKADE
RIJNSTRAAT
VECHTSTRAAT
CHURCHILLLAAN
DEURLOO-STRAAT
DIEPENBROCKSTRAAT
H. HEIJERMANSWEG
HARINGVLIETSTR.
SCHELDESTRAAT
DINTELSTRAAT
MAASSTRAAT
WAALSTRAAT
ROOSEVELTLAAN
LEKSTRAAT
WIELINGENSTRAAT
EUROPAPLEIN
RAI Tentoonstelling en Congresgebouw
UITERWAARDENSTRAAT

Rijksmuseum

location 1 Jan Luijkenstraat, 020 6747000, rijksmuseum.nl * tram 2 and 5 (stop Rijksmuseum), 3, 12, 16 and 24 (stop Museumplein) * open daily 9 am - 6 pm * admission € 14, under 18 years free

The Rijksmuseum is the largest and most important National Museum of the Netherlands. Officially it is called the Rijksmuseum Amsterdam, but Dutch people just call it the Rijksmuseum (pronounce as 'ryksmuseum'). We are sure that both you and your parents will be surprised of the grandeur of the building. It was in fact the famous architect Pieter Cuypers who designed the building in the 19th century and he was also responsible for designing Amsterdam Central Station. Recently the museum was completely **renovated** and the project took the architect and builders over ten years! At the museum you can mainly see paintings from the 15th century until the 19th century, with an emphasis on the Dutch masters of the 17th century (see also the Golden Age on page 42). The most important painters are Rembrandt van Rijn, Frans Hals, Johannes Vermeer and Jan Steen. The most famous painting in the Rijksmuseum is the **Night Watch** by Rembrandt van Rijn. Also famous is **The Milkmaid** by Johannes Vermeer.

The Night Watch

Does this sound a bit boring? No worries, because there are all kinds of activities in the Rijksmuseum especially for children and families. The **Rijksmuseum Multimedia Tour** (also in English) for example, now includes a family game inviting you to solve eight fascinating Rijksmuseum mysteries. It takes about one hour and if you succeed, there is a surprise waiting at the end of the tour. The game is for two to four persons, each using their own device. Apart from the various family activities there are also numerous workshops and other activities. Design your own Rijksmuseum phone case for example, learn how to make an etching or take a series of photographs of the Rijksmuseum. The activities are usually designed for Dutch children from 6 years and older but most of the time the workshop leaders also speak English. And did we mention the lovely museum shop? Definitely take a look inside!

Tips!

Often you have to wait in line at the entrance of the Rijksmuseum. April, May and August are the busiest months and the wait can be up to thirty minutes. Friday, Saturday and Sunday are usually also very busy. Arriving before 10 am or after 3 pm means less waiting time. It is also useful to buy an e-ticket in advance because then you do not have to get past the ticket office. Great fun: after visiting the Rijksmuseum rent a pedalo Canal Bike. The rental pier is practically on the doorstep of the Rijksmuseum. For more information see page 31.

REMBRANDT VAN RIJN PAINTED THE NIGHT WATCH BETWEEN 1639 AND 1642. IT USED TO HANG IN THE MAIN HALL OF AMSTERDAM'S KLOVENIERSDOELEN AND IN 1715 IT MOVED TO THE TOWN HALL ON DAM SQUARE. BECAUSE IT WAS HANGING IN BETWEEN TWO DOORS A STRIP AT THE TOP AND LEFT SIDE HAD TO BE CUT OFF. WHAT A SHAME! BECAUSE THE PAINTING IS STILL SO ENORMOUS IT CANNOT BE EASILY REMOVED IN CASE OF AN EMERGENCY. THEREFORE THE MUSEUM HAS A SEPARATE NARROW PASSAGE SOLELY FOR THE PAINTING. DURING WORLD WAR 2 THE NIGHT WATCH WAS HIDDEN IN A CAVE NEAR THE CITY OF MAASTRICHT. WHEN THE PAINTING RETURNED TO THE MUSEUM IN 1945 THE MUSEUM DIRECTOR WAS SO HAPPY THAT HE ACCIDENTALLY FELL ON TOP OF IT. FORTUNATELY THERE WAS NOT TOO MUCH DAMAGE.

Van Gogh Museum

location 7 Paulus Potterstraat 7, 020 5705200, vangoghmuseum.nl * tram 2, 3, 5 and 12 (stop Van Baerlestraat), 16 and 24 (stop Museumplein) * open Mar-Aug daily 9 am - 6 pm, Fri until 10 pm; Sep-Dec daily 9 am - 5 pm, Fri until 10 pm * admission € 15, under 17 years free

When you look at the name of this museum you can probably already guess what it is about. Indeed, this museum is about Vincent van Gogh. But who was Vincent van Gogh and why was he so important that there is a whole museum crammed with his work? Let's start at the very beginning. Vincent was born in 1853 and he got five brothers and sisters. Theo was his favorite brother. At school Vincent was very good at speaking foreign languages but at the age of fifteen he quit school and started working in an art gallery in The Hague, later followed by one in London. He got increasingly interested in drawings and paintings, but only when he was 27 years old he decided to become an artist. He moved to Brussels and regularly got money from his brother because he himself didn't make a dime. For almost eighteen years the two brothers wrote extensive lettres to each other.

Dark colours

At the start of his painting career Vincent called himself a peasant's painter since he used only pretty dark coulours. These colours were very different from the light shades that were at that time fashionable in Paris. Sometimes he took painting lessons but that never lasted long because he easily got bored. In 1886 he moved to Paris where his brother Theo lived. In Paris Vincent started to use a lot more colour and in that time he painted many self-portraits. In 1888 Vincent moved to Provence, a region in the south of France. In Provence he painted his world famous still lifes of sunflowers (see the picture on one of the previous pages) and numerous other paintings. He was often joined by his painter friend Gauguin. But Vincent was not always happy. One day he and Gauguin started quarreling, and Vincent threatened Gauguin with a razor. Later he also cut off a piece of his own left ear, and he was brought to the hospital. When he came out of the hospital, Vincent was very miserable and he let himself get hospitalized in a mental institution. There he made a studio from his cell where he painted a hundred and fifty paintings.

One painting a day

In 1890 he moved to Auvers-sur-Oise, a small town near Paris, and here he painted nearly a painting a day. Halfway through the year Vincent once again did not feel well, and he shot himself in the chest. Two days later he died. At that time the paintings of Vincent van Gogh were not so popular. He has painted only for ten years but is considered to be one of the greatest Dutch painters. Mainly because he dared to experiment and did what he wanted. The Van Gogh Museum was opened in 1973 and houses the world's largest collection of works by Vincent van Gogh.

The Museumplein

Vincent's Travelling Case

Perhaps you can recognize certain aspects of his life story when looking at the paintings in the museum. On the website you can find even more information about his life, and also nice colouring pages and instructions for making a (digital) diorama. In the museum you can ask for Vincent's Travelling Case at the Information Desk (in Dutch and in English). This case is packed with fun assignments for children and these will help you to explore Vincent van Gogh's paintings. Are all the cases already been taken? Then try the free Treasure Hunt instead. If you go back afterwards and have them check your answers, they will give you a little gift. And do you come on weekends? Every Saturday and Sunday there are workshops for children aged 6 to 12 years (7,50 euros). It is perhaps also fun to download the free Touch Van Gogh app, and as of the end of 2014 there is even more. What about a Multimedia Tour for families. Enjoy!

Stedelijk Museum

location 10 Museumplein, 020 5732911, stedelijk.nl * tram 2, 3, 5 and 12 (stop Van Baerlestraat), 16 and 24 (stop Museumplein) * open daily 10 am - 8 pm, Thu until 10 pm * admission € 15, under 18 years free

It seems like all the museums on and around the Museumplein have been renovated in recent years. Apart from the Van Gogh Museum and the Rijksmuseum, the Stedelijk Museum is also severely remodelled. From the outside you will probably immediately notice the large new museum shop. You must definitely browse through all the fun stuff that is for sale. When you want to visit the museum itself be prepared to wait in line. Buying an e-ticket through the website ensures that you can use the fast lane.

Contemporary art

What can you see in the Stedelijk Museum? The Stedelijk Museum is the largest museum for modern and contemporary art and design in the Netherlands. This means that there is only art on display from about 1860 until now. We mention a few famous names: Karel Appel, Piet Mondriaan, Philippe Starck and Andy Warhol. By art we mean paintings and sculptures, but also jewelery, fashion, furniture, and photos. There is a permanent collection and in addition there are always temporary exhibitions.

Family Tours

With the Family Audio Visual Tour you and your family can discover all the highlights and surprises that the collection of the Stedelijk Museum has to offer. This tour is accompanied by audio and visual material, and is available in Dutch or English. Curious visitors aged 6 to 12 can visit the new studios on Sunday afternoon and take a special workshop with an artist or designer. These workshops are in Dutch but most workshop leaders probably also speak English. Also fun: the Family Lab. The walls of the Family Lab are ready: 141,570 Lego pieces are waiting for your hands and creativity. Where will you put which colour? Think about shapes of colour, and proportions and work in 3D.

TIP! THE STEDELIJK RESTAURANT ON THE GROUND FLOOR IS A GOOD PLACE FOR BREAKFAST, LUNCH OR JUST A DRINK. WHEN THE WEATHER IS NICE YOU CAN SIT ON THE TERRACE. THE RESTAURANT IS DAILY OPENED FROM 8.30 AM UNTIL MIDNIGHT.

SOME PEOPLE IN AMSTERDAM SAY THAT THE RENEWED MUSEUM RESEMBLES A BATHTUB. LOOK AT THE PICTURE. WHAT DO YOU THINK?

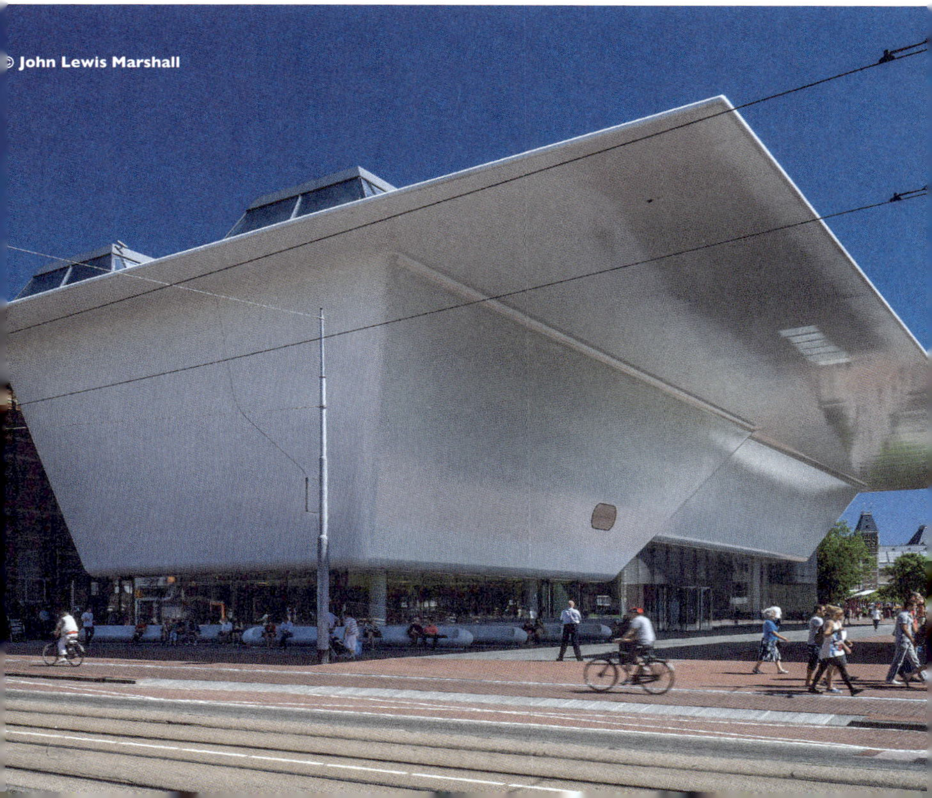
© John Lewis Marshall

Royal Concertgebouw

location 10 Concertgebouwplein, conertgebouw.nl * tram 2 (stop Van Baerlestraat), 5, 16 and 24 (stop Museumplein) * open free concerts at lunch time on Wednesdays at 12.30 pm

The Royal Concertgebouw (concert hall) exists for over 125 years and is one of the most famous concert halls in the world. This is mainly because of the beautiful quality of the sound of the music that is being played. You can tour the building with a guided tour, but we can imagine that this is a little boring. Rather visit a free lunch concert on Wednesday afternoons. This allows you to really see and hear the beauty of a concert hall orchestra. Check the website for more information.

Goochem Wooden Toys

location 80 1e Constantijn Huygensstraat, 020 6124704, goochem.nl * tram 1 (stop Eerste Constantijn Huygensstraat), 2 and 5 (stop Leidseplein), 17 (stop Bilderdijkstraat) * open Mon 1 pm - 6 pm, Tue-Fri 9.30 am - 6 pm, Sat 9.30 am - 5 pm

This store is within walking distance of the Rijksmuseum and the Van Gogh Museum and mainly sells (self made) wooden toys. If you are allowed to bring something home from Amsterdam, definitely stop by to look for something original. In addition there are also children's furniture, books, toy trains, musical instruments and games sold. Online you can have a look but also order gifts (in case your bag or suitcase is too small).

Vondelpark

location main entrance at Stadhouderskade, vondelpark.nl * tram 1, 2, 3, 5, 10 and 12 (stop Leidseplein)

The Vondelpark is the most famous and, with annually about ten million visitors, also the most popular park in Amsterdam. This is not so strange considering the fact that the park is located in the centre of the city, is very green and there are a lot of things you can do. The park is also quite large, about 2 kilometers long and 400 metres wide. The park was developed in 1864 and a year later it opened to the public. By then it was not yet known as 'Vondelpark' but people called it the 'New Park'. When in 1867 a statue of the poet Vondel was placed in the park it got its present name. The statue is still there, maybe you can try and find it. When the weather is nice bring a well-stocked picnic basket and a football along and take a peek at all the ordinary and less than ordinary people surrounding you. The park was designed in the English landscape style. This means that the park is as natural as possible without neatly trimmed hedges and neat flower beds, and you are allowed to walk on the grass. But what can you do at the Vondelpark? You can play soccer, sunbathe, picnic, go skating or bring a visit to the Open Air Theatre.

Vondelpark Open Air Theatre

Every summer (May-Sep) there are shows in the Vondelpark Open Air Theatre and the programme changes daily. On Friday, Saturday and Sunday there is dance, cabaret and music, and there are plays and special performances for children. The performances are free and the programme can be found on Openluchttheater.nl. Do you want to be sure you have a good spot? Through the website you can reserve some seats for every show. These seats cost 5 euros.

TIP! FANCY A PICNIC IN THE VONDELPARK? AT PICKNICKVONDELPARK.NL YOU CAN ORDER A PICNIC BASKET WITH ALL KINDS OF YUMMY GOODIES.

Boomkroonpad and more

Approximately halfway through the park you can also explore the top of the trees on the relatively new 'Boomkroonpad' that winds through the treetops. Small children can enjoy themselves playing in the children's pond; older kids go to the playground at the park entrance on the Amstelveenseweg, at the Vondeltuin restaurant. There are also four smaller playgrounds in the park and animal lovers can go in search of squirrels, storks, toads, salamanders and frogs that live in the greenery. And maybe you encounter the Vondel Gnome. He is fairly new and asks everyone to clean up their mess.

SEVERAL WORLD RECORDS ARE BROKEN IN THE VONDELPARK. ONE OF THE BEST IS THE WORLD RECORD 'PICNICKING WITH MANY PEOPLE'. IN THE GUINNESS BOOK OF RECORDS YOU CAN READ THAT IN 2009, 352 PEOPLE ATTENDED A PICNIC.

NOWADAYS A LOT OF PEOPLE CYCLE THROUGH THE PARK, BUT IN THE BEGINNING THIS WAS NOT ALLOWED. FROM 1893 IT WAS ONLY PERMITTED TO CYCLE IN THE MORNING.

ARE YOU A GOOD SKATER? THEN JOIN THE FRIDAY NIGHT SKATE. THIS POPULAR TOUR (APPROX. 20 KM) BEGINS IN THE VONDELPARK AND TAKES YOU THROUGH AMSTERDAM. EVERYONE STARTS AT 8:30 PM AT THE FORMER FILM MUSEUM.

The Blauwe Theehuis

The Blauwe Theehuis

location **Vondelpark, near the entrance at the Van Eeghenstraat, 020 6620254, blauwetheehuis.nl** * **tram** **1, 2 or 5 (stop Eerste Constantijn Huygensstraat or Van Baerlestraat)** * **open** **Mon-Fri 9 am - 5 pm, Sat + Sun 9 am - 8 pm**

This round building was built around seventy years ago. From the huge terrace below and the upper terrace (a total of 700 seats!) you have a wonderful view of the surrounding greenery. You can drink coffee, have lunch or dinner and occasionally there are live performances. Children can choose all kinds of delicious goodies from the menu. A peanut butter sandwich for example, or a roll with hazelnut paste. But we would order the homemade apple pie! From Thursday to Sunday The Blauwe Theehuis is also open for dinner.

Groot Melkhuis

location **2 Vondelpark 2, 020 6129674, grootmelkhuis.nl** * **tram** **1, 2 or 5 (stop Eerste Constantijn Huygensstraat or Van Baerlestraat)** * **open** **daily from 10 am** * **admission** **children's workshops € 5**

At the Groot Melkhuis restaurant your parents can sit back and relax on the terrace for hours, because you will certainly not want to leave. For children aged 4 to 12 years, there is a good and large playground, even with an electric helicopter. Every weekend in summer you can bounce in a huge bouncy castle or order something sweet at the candy floss stall. Furthermore, every Wednesday afternoon there are children's workshop from 2 pm to 4 pm where you can draw, paint or craft. Your little brother or sister will enjoy himself/herself in the sandbox.

The Children's Cooking Cafe

location 6B Vondelpark (at the Kattenlaantje), 020 6253257, kinderkookkafe.nl * tram 1, 2 or 5 (stop Eerste Constantijn Huygensstraat or Van Baerlestraat) * open daily 10 am - 5 pm * admission Help-Yourself-Bar depends on the ingredients used, from € 1,50, Open Diner € 12,50 per child and € 12,50 per guest

About thirty years ago three neighbours started the Children's Cooking Café (Kinderkookkafé), where children do all the cooking and serving. Daily between 10 am and 5 pm you can walk in to build sausage bugs, create cucumber puzzles, make milkshakes and pizzas or to bake cookies. Just fetch all the ingredients you need at the Help-Yourself-Bar. You don't know what you are looking for? Just look at the images and you know immediately what stuff you have to pick. You then go to work and if necessary, there are people around to give you a hand. Your parents in the meantime can enjoy a cup of coffee and a delicious piece of cake that other children have made the day before. Every first Saturday of the month an open dinner is organized. Children aged 7 years and older can register in advance and prepare a delicious meal for their parents and other guests. Brothers, sisters, fathers, mothers, grandfathers and grandmothers: anyone can join. The cooks start at 3.30 pm with the cooking, guests arrive at 6 pm. The idea is that you are not only cooking, but you are also serving the food and pouring drinks. For the Help -Yourself-Bar you do not have to make a reservation (except if you want to come with more than five children), for an Open Diner a reservation is required.

Imps and Elfs

location 41-44 Sloterkade, 020 3460200, imps-elfs.nl * tram 1 and 17 (stop Surinameplein) * open Mon-Fri 9.30 am - 6 pm, Sat 9.30 am - 5 pm

The Dutch clothing brand Imps & Elfs is sold all over the world, but the main office is in South Amsterdam. The clothing is 100% child labour free and made from organic cotton. So plenty of reasons for your parents to get excited. This store used to be a garage, and maybe you can still see that.

The Hollandsche Manege

location 140 Vondelstraat, 020 6180942, dehollandschemanege.nl * tram 1 (stop Eerste Constantijn Huygenstraat) * open daily 10 am - 5 pm * admission € 8, 3-12 years € 4

On an almost secret location near the Vondelpark you can find the Hollandsche Manege. This is the oldest riding-school in the Netherlands, and people are riding horses here since 1744. You can have a look inside by entering through an inconspicuous door at the Vondelstraat. Admire the horses but also the beautiful old building. In the Living Horse Museum (the Levend Paardenmuseum in Dutch) you will learn all about the history of this riding-school. Check out what people in the old days used to wear while riding and watch an interesting film about the history of the riding-school. By doing the quest (2.50 euros) you will learn all about horses and horse riding. Of course you can also take riding lessons, but that is ony convenient if you are living near Amsterdam.

Helden en Boeven

location 27H Bosboom Toussaintstraat, 020 4274407, heldenboeven.nl * tram 1, 2 and 5 (stop Leidseplein), 17 (stop Elandsgracht) * open Tue-Fri 10 am - 6 pm, Sat 10 am - 5 pm

Helden en Boeven is not just a children's bookstore, but also a small movie theatre and a gift shop, and throughout the year various fun activities are being organized. Twice a week new books are being delivered and they are all read by the bookloving staff. So do not hesitate to ask for recommendations. The gifts that are sold all have something to do with books. What about a Gruffalo cuddly toy? Every Wednesday you can watch short films with lemonade, popcorn or a biscuit. During school holidays more films are being screened, just look at the calendar on the website. In this calendar you can also see what other activities are on the programme. A Father's Day breakfast in your pyjama for example.

Olympic Experience

location 2 Olympisch Stadion, 020 6711115, olympischstadion.nl * tram 16 (stop Olympisch Stadion) * open Tue-Sun 11 am - 5 pm * admission € 6, 5-12 years € 5, tour € 12,50 (incl. entrance to the Olympic Experience)

Do you like sports? Then it is nice to visit the Amsterdam Olympic Stadium. In this beautiful, old stadium,the Olympic Games were held in 1928. In the visitor centre you can visit the Olympic Experience, where you are taken back in time but also to the future of Dutch sports. You can watch television images of all kinds of sports, take a selfie on the centre spot of the football field and admire the Wall of Fame with all Dutch medal winners.

Amsterdamse Bos

location main entrance at the Amstelveenseweg (near the Van Nijenrodeweg), 020 5456100, amsterdamsebos.nl * bus 170 and 172 (stop Koenenkade, Kalfjeslaan or Van Nijenrodeweg)

This forest is located in the south of Amsterdam, on the border with Amstelveen. It is very large and every year it attracts 6 million visitors. Start by picking up a free map at the **visitor centre the Boswinkel**, near the main entrance at the Van Nijenrodeweg. Every Sunday fun familiy activities are being organized here, such as sifting through owl pellets and making a tree passport. You can also book excursions and tours. For example go along with a forester on a electrical boat and discover the winding waters of the forest. A reservation is required.

Relaxing & recharging

You can sit back and relax at the **Grand Café Bosbaan**, where you have a beautiful view of the famous track where large regattas are being held. This café is not the only place where you can eat or drink. **Boerderij Meerzicht** is also a nice (pancake) address. After a walk through the woods enjoy a delicious pancake with nuts and powdered sugar for example. In summer there are also several kiosks in the forest. *For more information bosbaan.nl and boerderijmeerzicht.nl*

Water fun

The swimming water in the Amsterdamse Bos is clean enough to take a swim. At several places you can have fun in the water. For the little ones the **small and large children's pools** are filled with water when the temperature reaches 20 degrees Celsius. Both pools are surrounded by picnic benches and there are a playground, restrooms and a shop where you can buy food and drinks. There is also an official bathing site in the forest, the **Great Pond** (Grote Vijver in Dutch), with a separate swimming area. Since 2014 there are islands for playing created in the pond. This playing area was designed by pupils of an Amsterdam school. There are bridges in the water, ropes, poles to climb in, and nets and rafts. In addition, you can build huts, have a picnic or just lie in the sun. Do you have questions about swimming in the Amsterdamse Bos? Then call the Boswinkel at 020 5456100.

Miniport

Miniport is one of the new attractions in the forest. On the big pond in the Amsterdamse Bos children (4 years and older) can feel like a real captain and operate their own boat. You will also learn everything about boats. How does hydropower work for example, and do you know how to make knots? When picking your own boat you can choose between a police boat, a lifeboat or a cruise ship and you are allowed to sail for 15 or 30 minutes.
Miniport is closed in winter, the rest of the year you are welcome on weekends, on Wednes-

day afternoon and during school holidays. *For more information and opening hours see miniportworld.com*

Fun Forest

In this park you can climb like a real Tarzan and swing through the trees. At a height of 4 to 15 metres, you can take different routes. You use lianas, aerial runways, rope ladders and other climbing aids. For children there are different routes they can do alone. Older children can take other routes, but only under the accompaniment of an adult. Note: it is not allowed to climb with flip flops or sandals, so make sure you take proper shoes with you. In winter the park is closed, but is is always useful to look at the website in advance to see if it is open. *For more information visit funforest.nl*

Ridammerhoeve goat farm

In the middle of the Amsterdamse Bos you can find the Ridammerhoeve goat farm. You can have a (free) look at the stables and at the farm you can buy vegetables and herbs from the garden. There is also a playground and we advise you to order the delicious pancakes! *For more information see geitenboerderij.nl*

Open air theatre

Yearly from July to September, five days a week, the Bostheater organizes a play in the open air theatre of the forest. There are also activities and performances specifically for children.

When you go to the theatre make sure to bring something to eat or buy one of the picnic baskets. Tip: it can be very busy at the theatre, especially when nice weather is predicted, so if you want to have a seat make sure you are on time. *For more information see bostheater.nl*

ON SUNDAY YOU CAN TRAVEL WITH A RESTORED ANTIQUE TRAM TO THE AMSTERDAMSE BOS. THE TRAM DEPARTS FROM THE HAARLEMMERMEERSTATION AND DRIVES TO AMSTELVEEN. THIS TRIP TAKES ABOUT HALF AN HOUR, BUT IF YOU GET OFF AT THE FOREST THE JOURNEY IS SHORTER. SEE MUSEUMTRAMLIJN.ORG.

AMSTELPARK

location main entrance at the Europaboulevard near the A.J. Ernststraat; there are four other entrances, amstelpark.info and speeltuin-amstelpark.nl * On foot a 7-minute walk from the RAI train station * open daily from 8 am

The Amstelpark was built in 1972 for the Floriade which was then held in Amsterdam. The Floriade is an important international horticultural exhibition organized every ten years somewhere in the Netherlands. In the Amstelpark is a lot to see and do. There are sand pits, climbing frames, roundabouts, slides, bumper cars and cable cars. For younger children there is a separate playing area with sandpits and playing equipment.

Midget golf

There are two different courses at Midgetgolf Amstelpark. Both have 18 holes, but one course is laid out on grass and resembles a real golf course with bunkers, slopes and water. *For more information midgetgolf-amstelpark.nl*

The Bastion

The Bastion is located next to the petting zoo. You can step into a bumper boat, drive on a mini scooter, dig with an excavator, and there is also an outlet for ice cream, drinks and tasty snacks. *For more information see speeltuin-amstelpark.nl*

City Farm

After a major renovation in 2010 the petting zoo of the Amstelpark is now called the City Farm (Stadsboerderij in Dutch). You can visit all kinds of animals like little horses, pot-bellied pigs, chickens, goats, rabbits and guinea pigs. You can not only look at them, on Wednesday you can also cuddle the animals. In addition there are various activities being organized such as a sheep shearing festival in spring. You will also find a stork's nest in the park, a meadow with Scottish Highlanders and a bat cellar.

And there is even more

Take a ride in the Amsteltrain that will bring you past the Rosarium (a rose garden with up to 160 different types of roses), the Rhododendron Valley (8000 rhododendrons of 139 species) and the Riekermolen mill. Tickets can be purchased at the station near the main entrance. Furthermore IVN Amsterdam has a visitor centre in the Amstelpark: the Rietschuur. IVN is an organisation promoting the exploration of urban nature. Once a month IVN organizes special children's activities. *For more information see ivn.nl*

WEST AMSTERDAM

The western part of Amsterdam used to be a bit of a boring neighbourhood. But around twenty years ago all the houses were renovated and the Westerpark and its surrounding grounds got a facelift. Nowadays West Amsterdam is hot and happening and everyone wants to live, play and relax here. So explore the west: discover the secrets of the greenery, built a raft, play in the water and spot all kinds of creepy critters.

Candy made by Papabubble

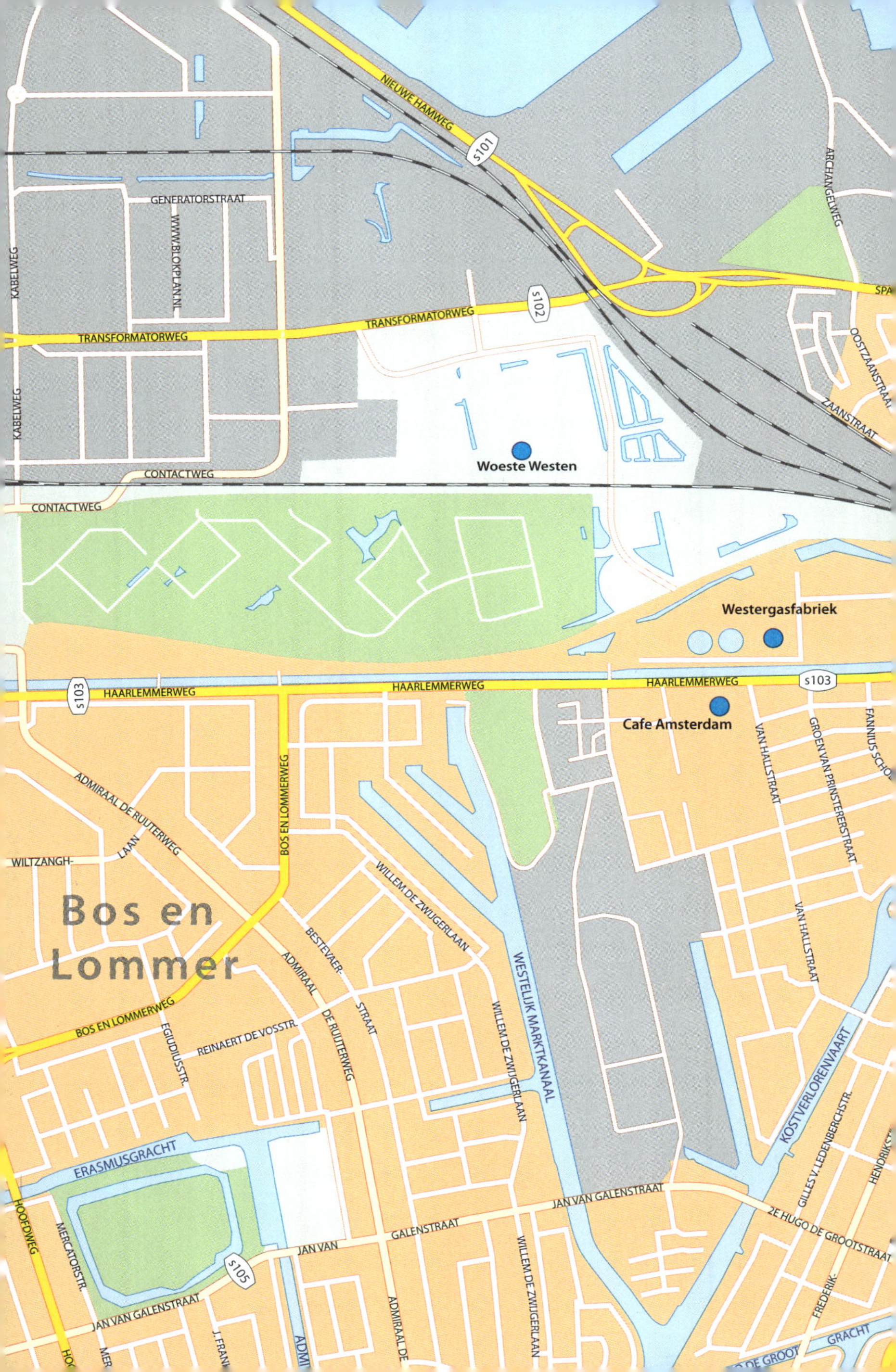
NIEUWE HAMWEG
s101
GENERATORSTRAAT
WWW.BLOKPLAN.NL
KABELWEG
ARCHANGELWEG
s102
TRANSFORMATORWEG
TRANSFORMATORWEG
OOSTZAANSTRAAT
ZAANSTRAAT
KABELWEG
Woeste Westen
CONTACTWEG
CONTACTWEG
Westergasfabriek
s103
HAARLEMMERWEG
HAARLEMMERWEG
HAARLEMMERWEG
s103
Cafe Amsterdam
VAN HALLSTRAAT
GROEN VAN PRINSTERERSTRAAT
ADMIRAAL DE RUITERWEG
BOS EN LOMMERWEG
WILTZANGH-
LAAN
WILLEM DE ZWIJGERLAAN
Bos en Lommer
BESTEVAER-
STRAAT
ADMIRAAL
DE RUITERWEG
VAN HALLSTRAAT
WESTELIJK MARKTKANAAL
WILLEM DE ZWIJGERLAAN
BOS EN LOMMERWEG
EGIDIUSSTR.
REINAERT DE VOSSTR.
KOSTVERLORENVAART
GILLES V. LEDENBERCHSTR.
ERASMUSGRACHT
JAN VAN GALENSTRAAT
2E HUGO DE GROOTSTRAAT
HOOFDWEG
MERCATORSTR.
JAN VAN
GALENSTRAAT
WILLEM DE ZWIJGERLAAN
s105
JAN VAN GALENSTRAAT
FREDERIK-
GRACHT

Het IJ
Het IJ
HOUTHAVEN
Westerpark
Jordaan
Centraal Station
St. Nicolaaskerk
Schreierstoren
Ronde Lutherse Kerk
Papabubble
Noordermarkt
Anne Frank Museum
Westerkerk
Kinderboekwinkel
Villa Zeezicht
Nieuwe Kerk
Koninklijk Paleis
Dam
Met. Deli
Oude Kerk
China Town
TASMANSTRAAT
NOVA ZEMBLASTRAAT
VAN DIEMENSTRAAT
VAN NOORDT GRACHT
BARANTSZSTRAAT
ZOUTKEETSGRACHT
REALENGRACHT
ZANDHOEK
SLOTERDIJKSTRAAT
GROTE BICKERSSTRAAT
WESTERDOK
WESTERDOKSDIJK
WESTERKANAAL
HOUTMANKADE
SPAARNDAMMERSTRAAT
PLANCIUSSTRAAT
EILANDSGRACHT
HAARLEMMERPLEIN
HAARLEMMER HOUTTUINEN
HAARLEMMERDIJK
NWE. WAGENSTR.
BROUWERSGRACHT
NIEUWE WESTERDOKSTR.
DE RUIJTERKADE
PRINS HENDRIKKADE
SINGEL
SINGELGRACHT
MARNIXKADE
MARNIXSTRAAT
LIJNBAANSGRACHT
PALMGRACHT
WILLEMSSTRAAT
GOUDSBLOEMSTRAAT
LINDENGRACHT
LINDENSTRAAT
BOOMSTRAAT
WESTERSTRAAT
ANJELIERSSTRAAT
TUINSTRAAT
EGELANTIERSSTRAAT
EGELANTIERSGRACHT
NIEUWE LELIESTRAAT
BLOEMGRACHT
BLOEMSTRAAT
ROZENGRACHT
RAADHUISSTRAAT
PALEISSTR.
PRINSENGRACHT
KEIZERSGRACHT
HERENGRACHT
LEIDSEGRACHT
PRINSENSTRAAT
HERENSTRAAT
LANGESTRAAT
KORSJESPOORTSTEEG
BLAUWBURGW.
BERGSTR.
SPUISTRAAT
NIEUWEZIJDS VOORBURGWAL
NIEUWENDIJK
DAMRAK
ZEEDIJK
GELDERSEKADE
OUDE KERKSPL.
WARMOESSTRAAT
BEURSSTR.
ST. JANSSTR.
STORMST.
KROMME WAAL
WAALSEILANDSGRACHT
RECHT BOOMSSLOOT
DRIE KONINGEN STR.
TOLHUISKANAAL
GRASWEG
DISTELWEG
ASTERWEG
GEVLEWEG
BUIKSLOOT
s102
s100

Culture Park Westergasfabriek

location Polonceaukade, westergasfabriek.nl * bus 21 and tram 10 (stop Van Hallstraat)

This culture park is actually a mix of a park, several restaurants, small shops and art galleries. Many of these are not really interesting for children, but the city park is a must. It is located on the outskirts of the city. There are all kinds of activities, you can picnic, play in the water and there is a relaxed atmosphere. Parents can sit at one of the lovely terraces and there is free WiFi throughout the park.

Ketelhuis

This is a special cinema because it plays only Dutch films. There is a special Youth Film Passport with all kinds of games, but you can also collect stamps in it. Children pay 7,50 euros. *For more information see ketelhuis.nl*

Children's pond

The Westerpark has a great children's pond which is refilled every morning with fresh tap water. Dogs are not allowed and the use of glassware is prohibited, so you can walk safely. *The children's pond is open from May until October*

Petting zoo

In the western part of the park, behind the walking and cycling path, you will find a petting zoo. There are some special animals living in the zoo like a giant pig (Motti), a cow, goats (with very short legs), chicken and more. You can also have a drink and regulary there are activities organized like a sheep shearers feast, a living nativity scene and a Sinterklaas ceebration. *Open Tue-Sun 9 am - 5 pm*

Renting a boat

Do you want to explore the water? Rent an environmentally friendly boat at Boats4rent. The boats are suitable for up to six people and within fifteen minutes you are in the Amsterdam canals. The boats are easy to handle, work on green electricity and when renting a boat you will receive a good water map with nice suggestions. Renting a boat is possible from 79 euros for three hours. When the weather predictions are good it is convenient to make a reservation in advance. You can find the boat rental alongside De Bakkerswinkel where you can buy some goodies to eat on board. *For more informatie see bootjehureninamsterdam.com*

De Bakkerswinkel

De Bakkerswinkel is located at the entrance of the Culture Park Westergasfabriek. You can eat both inside and outside, and on the menu are all kinds of homemade sandwiches and sweets. All items are also suitable for take-away so you can enjoy them in the park.

Order delicious breakfast sandwiches (for example with homemade jam or local cheese), quiche, cake, salads, fresh juices, and coffee. All ingredients are organic and the food is as homemade as possible. *For more information see debakkerswinkel.nl (branch Amsterdam-West)*

And there is even more

If you visit the website of the Westergasfabriek you can see that there is much more to be done. There are for example several playgrounds, there is a Whispering Bank, you can picnic on the platforms in the gas tank ponds and at the nice and relaxed Westergasterras almost weekly kids' activities are being organized.

PAPABUBBLE

location 70 Haarlemmerdijk, 020 6262662, papabubble.nl * on foot the shop is within walking distance of Amsterdam Central Station * open Mon 1 pm - 6 pm, closed on Tue, Wed-Fri 11 am - 6 pm, Sun noon - 5 pm

On the Haarlemmerdijk near Culture Park Westerpark you can find one of the branches of candy workshop Papabubble. Here they make candy on the spot, right in the middle of the store. If you want you can ask questions at the candy makers and of course you can buy and taste some handmade candy. Recently Papabubble has also opened an online shop; a good idea for children looking for an original gift for thier friends.

Woeste Westen

location **3 Overbrakerpad, woestewesten.nl** * **bus** **21 and** **tram** **10 (stop Van Hallstraat), bus 48 (stop Spaarndammerdijk)** * **open** **always** * **admission** **free**

If you prefer to stay clean and dry, then this natural playground is not your cup of tea. At the Woeste Westen you can build huts, sail on rafts, search for frogs, climb trees and play in the mud. There is a lot of water with reeds, bushes, shrubs and sand. The people of the Woeste Westen prefer that you come and play without your parents, but in that case you have to be older than 7 years and have a swimming certificate. This playground is located in the Westerpark, near the Westergasfabriek. You can come here every day and often a playground leader is present, namely on Wednesday, Saturday and Sunday from 11 am to 6 pm, and on other days from noon to 6 pm. You can also buy drinks and some small goodies.

Cafe Amsterdam

location **6 Watertorenplein, 020 6822666, cradam.nl** * **bus** **21 and** **tram** **10 (stop Van Hallstraat)** * **open** **daily from 10.30 am**

This definitely is a family friendly restaurant, as there even is a special children's menu. Eat delicious fries with applesauce and croquettes, spring rolls or sausages. Pasta or hamburgers are also possible. Previously, this restaurant was a pump house and until 1996 the machines operated at full speed. Outside you can see a huge white water tower. Maybe now you understand why this square is called the Water Tower Square (Watertorenplein in Dutch). Have you finished eating? Start drawing or walk around and see if there is something going on. It is almost inevitable that there are other children present. Go before or after you visit the restaurant to the Culture Park Wetergasfabriek across the street (see page 142).

The Ontdekhoek

location **145 Burgemeester Röellstraat, 020 4116846, ontdekhoek.nl** * **metro** **50 (stop Jan van Galenstraat),** **tram** **13 (stop Jan van Galenstraat)** * **open** **Wed, Fri, Sat and Sun 10 am - 5 pm** * **admission** **€ 10, adults € 8**

The Ontdekhoek is a large workshop where you can do all kinds of scientific experiments. It is a bit out of the city centre, but we found this place so rewarding that we still like to mention it. Have you always wanted to know how to make crisps out of a potato? Or how to develop photos in a dark room? And have you ever made your own soap? Go ahead and see for yourself how it can be done. Everything you make at the Ontdekhoek you can take home with you.

The Natureluur

location Sloterpark (next to the petting zoo), 4 President Allendelaan, 06 33306191, denatureluur.nl * bus 61 from the Sloterdijk train station (stop Oeverpad) * open always * admission free

At the Sloterpark you will find the public playground the Natureluur. It is a bit off the beaten track and when you plan on playing here it is advisable to wear old cloths. You can enjoy playing in and around water, there are all kinds of exciting playing equipment and if you pay a little attention you also learn a lot about nature. On the Facebook page of the Natureluur playground you can read which activities are on the programme. Building rafts for example, or catching water bugs, but also supping on the pond or cruising across the waters of the Sloterplas lake.

Construction playground 't Landje

location 1 Rembrandtpark, 020 6183604, impulskinderopvang.nl * tram 17 (stop Postjesweg), 13 (stop Admiraal Helfrichstraat) or metro 50 from the Amsterdam Sloterdijk train station (stop Jan van Galenstraat) * open Wed-Fri noon - 5 pm, Sat + Sun 10 am - 5 pm. During school holidays Wed-Sun 10 am - 5 pm * admission most activities are free

A few years ago Dutch newspaper Het Parool considered this playground to be the best playground in Amsterdam. And this doesn't surprise us at all. Because this is not just a playground, this is an adventurous playground. You can find 't Landje in the Rembrandtpark and who wants to build rafts or cabins must first take a cable car or ferry to the island where the playground is located. There you will find plenty of tools and wood so you can get started (under supervision). Do you not want to build or is it bad weather? Do not worry, there is a special indoor craft room, and you can also go canoeing, play table tennis, football or ride on a pony. Also fun: the treehouse from where you can slide down. For children under six years this is not really a suitable place.

TIP! AND WHEN YOU ARE IN THE REMBRANDTPARK ALSO TAKE A PEEK AT THE PETTING ZOO UYLENBURG. THIS IS ACTUALLY THE OLDEST PETTING ZOO IN AMSTERDAM (APART FROM THE ONE AT THE ARTIS ZOO). THERE IS ALSO A SMALL PLAYGROUND AND A SHOP TO BUY SOME YUMMY STUFF. MORE INFORMATION AT PETTINGUYLENBURG.NL.

ACTIVE & SPORTIVE

In Amsterdam there are a lot of interesting museums and other attractions, but sometimes you just want some action, like climbing, biking, boating, stepping or supping. And how about visiting a nice theatre? Or do you prefer a refreshing dive into the water?

BABBOE City
www.babboe.com

IN OR ON THE WATER

In the Kidskinfo chapter we already discussed a number of opportunities to explore Amsterdam by water. But there are other possibilities as you can read below. And did you know that the water in Amsterdam can not only be used as a means of transportation? You can also take a swim in it!

Renting a boat

Maybe you do not fancy a canal cruise, and rather plan your own route through the canals. In that case rent your own boat. There are several companies where you can rent a boat. The website Sloepdelen.nl is very useful (also in English) and here you can make a boat reservation. After making the reservation you will receive a code with which you can simply unlock one of the boats at the Nassaukade. Download a water map from the internet stating the rules of navigation. The boats of Mokum Boot are also at the Nassaukade. *See sloepdelen.nl, mokumboot.nl, bootjehureninamsterdam.com, amsterdamboothuren.nl*

DO YOU WANT TO PLAN YOUR OWN ROUTE THROUGH THE CANALS OR ARE YOU JUST WONDERING WHAT IS HAPPENING ON THE AMSTERDAM CANALS? PLEASE CHECK THE DIGITAL NAVIGATION MAP AT GRACHTEN.WATERNET.NL.

© RGB Stock

Supping

Do you really want to do something else, go for a SUP lesson through the Amsterdam canals. SUP stands for Stand Up Paddling and is originally from Hawaii. Normally you lie on your stomach on a surf board and you use your arms to paddle. With SUP you stand upright and use a paddle to move forward. Many celebrities also started supping because it is good for your body, singer Rihanna for example. M&M SUP organizes classes on IJburg (on the Blijburg beach) from April to October. You can also get private lessons or learn to SUP with a group of at least five people. Supping through the canals is also possible, but then you have to know the first important SUP tricks. Visit the Facebook page of SUP Amsterdam for photos and videos. Kanoschool.nl at the Admiralengracht also gives SUP lessons. *More information at mm-sup.com, kanoschool.nl and supcenter-amsterdam.nl*

Let's go for a swim

People looking for some refreshment can cool down at several places in the city. Go to one of the city beaches, a swimming pond or to a swimming pool.

Blijburg at Sea

You can find the Blijburg at Sea beach on IJburg, but the beach has moved a few times already. This is caused by the fact that there is a lot of building going on at IJburg, and Blijburg is always located at a spot where the ground has just been sprayed and where in the next few years houses will be built. When we wrote this guide Blijburg (version 3) was located near the bridge to Muiden and Weesp. At Blijburg you can swim, eat, drink, lie on the beach and enjoy yourself. There are also many activities for children. For example, on Sunday at eleven o'clock there is always a theatre show for everyone up to eight years, and there are children's workshops. Are you planning on going to Blijburg? Then check the website to see where it is currently located, and whether it is open that day. When the weather is not so nice the beach is closed on Monday and Tuesday, and in winter the opening hours vary. *For more information see blijburg.nl*

Strandzuid

Amsterdam is not situated right at the coastline but nevertheless there are plenty of beaches. There is also one between the RAI conference centre and the Beatrixpark called South Beach (Strandzuid in Dutch). This is a good place to relax with hammocks, lounge chairs, beach chairs and sand of course. So playing won't be a problem. Swimming is unfortunately not possible, but you can have a dip afterwards in the Beatrixpark. *For more information see strand-zuid.nl*

Swimming pools

There are several (indoor) swimming pools in Amsterdam and at the Zwembad-amsterdam.nl website you can find an overview. A popular pool is the **De Mirandabad** with indoor and outdoor pools and a pool with real waves. Upon entering anyone over 14 years old must identify themselves. So make sure your parents bring a passport or other means of identification. In the centre of Amsterdam you will find **The Marnix**, a sports centre with a pool. The pool has limited opening hours, but what makes this pool special is the fact that the water level in both pools is equal to the water level in the canal. That way you can look at the ducks and boats when swimming. The **Zuiderbad** near the Rijksmuseum is centrally located as well. Then there is also the **Sportfondsenbad** in East Amsterdam. This pool was built in the old Oostergasfabriek. Early 2015 North Amsterdam wil get a new swimming pool, the **Noorderparkbad** (see page 98). This pool replaces the Floraparkbad. *For more information see mirandabad.nl, hetmarnix.nl, zuid.amsterdam.nl, sportfondsen.nl*

Outdoor swimming

For those who want to swim outside we recommend the **Brediusbad** in the Spaarndammerbuurt. The heated outdoor pool is open from May to August. Another open-air swimming pool is the **Flevoparkbad** in Amsterdam-Oost (open daily from late April to early September). The **Optisport Zwembad Sloterparkbad** next to the Sloterplas lake has all kinds of indoor swimming facilities and in summer there is also a large outdoor area where you can swim, but there is a playground as well. *For more information see brediuszwembad.nl, flevoparkbad.nl, sloterparkbad.nl*

Paddling in the water

There are several places in Amsterdam where you can paddle in the water. In the **Beatrixpark** for example; a quiet and small park in the south of Amsterdam. Here you will find a playground, a sandbox and also a children's pool. This pool was once voted the best paddling pool in Amsterdam. You can also go to the paddling pool at the **Adelaarsweg** in the Noorderpark in the north of Amsterdam. This pool is filled with water when the thermometer reaches 20 degrees Celsius, and the water is changed daily. The pool is open in summer (if the weather permits it) daily from noon to 6 pm. Another lovely baby pool that is well hidden is the **Gibraltarbad** in the neighbourhood Bos en Lommer. We are told that even some local residents do not know of its existence. The municipality maintains the pool, there are toilets and usually there is supervision. The pool is located at the end of the Solebaystraat. *For more information see www.vriendenbeatrixpark.nl, noorderpark.amsterdam.nl*

DURING THE BATHING SEASON THERE IS A SCULPTURE OF A MERMAID AT THE EDGE OF THE POOL IN THE BEATRIXPARK. DE MERMAID HOLDS A SHELL FROM WHICH DRINKING WATER DRIPS INTO THE POOL. YOU ARE ALLOWED TO CLIMB ON THE SCULPTURE.

A natural swim

Do you want to swim in natural surroundings? Then go to the **Hoge Dijk**, a recreational area in Southeast Amsterdam. Here you can play in the water of the Playing Ditch. For older children there is a swimming beach. During the bathing season, from May 1 to October 1, the county inspects the water once every two weeks. In the **Amsterdamse Bos** you can swim as well on several locations. The Great Pond (Grote Vijver in Dutch) is surrounded by beautiful greenery and has a separate swimming area. You can aslo find Playing Islands in the pond with a beautiful water playground. See also page 134 for more information. *For more information visit De Boswinkel information centre in het Amsterdamse Bos, 020-545 6100 and www.groengebied-amstelland.nl*

Ride your bike

In the chapter with kids' information you could already read that you should pay attention when cycling in Amsterdam (see page 32), but where can you rent a bike? And what special bikes are there for rent? Let us surprise you!

Carrier cycles and more

A carrier cycle is not only original, you can also transport a few children in it (plus the necessary luggage). At **MacBike** you can rent a traditional carrier cycle (see page 4) or a cargo bike. Actually you can find many different types of bikes at MacBike, including children's bikes, tandems where a child sits at the front and child seats for regular bikes. Furthermore, this is the right place for making a guided tour by bike. MacBike rents bikes for 25 years and has seven branches in the city, including one at Amsterdam Central Station. At **WorkCycles** you can rent a family tandem for one adult and two children. Cargo bikes and carrier bikes are also for rent. WorkCycles has two branches, one in the Jordaan (at the Lijnbaansgracht) and one in Zeeburg (at the Veemarkt). *For more informayion see macbike.nl and workcycles.nl*

Guided tours

Of course you can plan your own biking trip through Amsterdam, but maybe it is a good idea to join an organized tour. **Amsterbike** organizes such tours, like a 3-hour tour through the historic city centre. Children's bikes and seats can be arranged. The guided tour is in English, so that won't be a problem. If it rains Amsterbike provides a nice rain cape. If you want to join a tour a reservation is required, and note that there are two meeting points. One at Amsterbike in the Piet Hein Garage of the Passenger Terminal Amsterdam, and one at the Public Library. Both are about a 10-minute walk from Amsterdam Central Station. If you want to travel by public transport, take tram 26 (direction IJburg) or tram 25 (direction Passenger Terminal), and get off at the stop Muziekgebouw/Bimhuis. *For more information see www.amsterbike.eu*

Bring a picnic

If you rent a bike at **Star Bikes** you can - in addition to your bike - also order a picnic basket or portable barbecue. Your parents can order the contents of the basket or barbecue set as well. Do not worry about the transportation of the picnic basket, because your parents can rent a special picnic bike. For children there are children's bikes and child seats. Are you already a little older? Than we would recommend the Street Rider. This typical bikes means you go kind of stepping through the city, and you have to use both of your legs. Take a look at the website to see what we mean. Then you can also see the Fun2Go bike, on which two riders sit next to each other. You can find Star Bikes behind Amsterdam Central Station, at 127 De Ruyterkade. *For more information see starbikesrental.com*

BMX Amsterdam

Take your own BMX or rent one and go crossing at the BMX tracks of BMX Amsterdam. Young and old, experienced or not, everyone can try it. Your father, mother, grandfather, aunt or sister must therefore also give it a go. You can go cycling on your own, but you can also join a clinic. Here you will learn the basics of riding a BMX bike. There are several clinics, but you must be with at least five people. Maybe you discover that you are really talented and who knows you will win a gold medal at the Olympics one day. *For more information see griffioenoutdoor.nl*

Scooter or skates

Okay, obviously it is not really a bike, but at the **Skate Dokter** you can rent skates or a scooter. When renting skates you also will get the necessary protective gear and those who can not skate can take lessons at the Skate Dokter. If you do not have much experience, the Skate Dokter recommends to avoid the city centre. A lot of fun and easy to do: go skating in the Vondelpark. From the shop at the Jan van Galenstraat it is a half hour walk to the park, by public transport it will take you 20 minutes. Are you with a group, then the Skate Dokter sometimes brings your gear to the park. *For more information see skatedokter.nl*

TIP: ARE YOU A GOOD SKATER? THEN JOIN THE FRIDAY NIGHT SKATE. THIS LARGE TOUR (ABOUT 20 KILOMETRES) STARTS IN THE VONDELPARK AND TAKES YOU THROUGH AMSTERDAM. EVERYONE GATHERS AT 8.30 PM AT THE ROUND BENCH AT THE FORMER FILM MUSEUM. LOOK FOR THE EXACT LOCATION ON THE WEBSITE FRIDAYNIGHTSKATE.COM.

Ice skating

Ice skating is typically Dutch. In very severe winters it occasionally happens that you can skate on the Amsterdam canals. But then it has to freeze severely during a few consecutive days. Only then the water circulation in a few places is shut down so that the canals can freeze. On the next page there are some good alternatives.

Edwin van Eis

Ice rinks

Around the holidays you can go to the ice rink at the **Westergasfabriek** in West Amsterdam. During the day it is very cozy, and afterwards you can have a nice drink at the Pacific Parc restaurant. From late November to late January you can also visit the energy efficient **Museumplein** ice rink. With the Rijksmuseum in the background it feels like you step into a romantic fairy tale. Of course there even is a good refreshment stall. From mid-November to early January, the **Leidseplein** turns into a real winter wonderland, including an ice skating rink, snow cannons, fritters and Christmas stalls. The **Jaap Eden Baan** is the most famous ice rink in Amsterdam. You can go ice skating for hours, both inside and outside. The rink is usually open from mid-October to late March and you can also take ice skating lessons, and enjoy some nice food and drinks. *For more information see pacificparc.nl, iceamsterdam.nl en jaapeden.nl*

THEATRE AND FILM

Do you enjoy dance, theatre, puppetry and film, then it might be a good idea to visit a theatre in Amsterdam. We made a list of some nice places where you can go and watch a show. Look in advance on the websites to see what's on and how to make a reservation.

The Krakeling

The Krakeling theatre exists for more than 35 years and is completely focused on children. There are many different types of performances on the programme, but the theatre is also suitable for birthday parties, workshops and stay-overs. Check the calender on the website to see what's on. The suitable ages are clearly indicated per show, and there are already shows for children two years of age. Also fun: on Sundays before or after the show you can make a Kids Cruise with your (grand) parents. You get on board at 30 Stadhouderskade, opposite the Holland Casino at the Max Euweplein. *For more information see krakeling.nl*

The Toverknol

Every Wednesday, Saturday and Sunday at 10.30 am, 12.15 pm and 2 pm you can go to the Toverknol to see a show. The nice thing is that everyone dresses up in advance. There are costumes available. So what do you want to be? A princess, knight or astronaut? Have some cookies and lemonade and enjoy the show! *For more information see detoverknol.nl*

The Koos Kneus Puppet Theatre

Koos Kneus has its own children's theatre in East Amsterdam. Every Wednesday afternoon and on Sundays he hosts puppet shows for children from two to four years and for children aged four to eight years. In the break and afterwards you can get your face painted and there are costumes to try on if you like. On the website you can read all about the different shows and for what age they are suitable. *For more informayion see kooskneus.nl*

The Amsterdam Marionette Theatre

The Amsterdam Marionette Theatre has plays for the young and old and music plays an important role in the shows. At the website you can read all about upcoming performances and whether they are suitable for children. Often there is also some background information for children about the show and sometimes you can even watch a film clip. We are curious what you think of it. *For more information see marionettentheater.nl*

Bijlmer Parktheater

The building of the Bijlmer Parktheater you simply can not miss. No wonder it was nominated for the Amsterdam Architecture Award. In this relatively new theatre four organizations join forces: Circus Elbow, Krater Theater, the Youth Theatre School and the Theaterwerkplaats. You can get all kinds of classes and workshops, there are festivals organized, dance and music performances and of course there is a lot of theatre on the programme. *For more information see bijlmerparktheater.nl*

Dutch Marionette Theatre

This theatre opened its doors in 1923. In that time marionette plays were completely unknown in the Netherlands. Therefore founder Bert Brugman started organizing shows in the attic of his parents' house. In 1930 the theatre got its own location and nowadays you can see a family show every Saturday and Sunday at 2 pm. Often the shows are adaptions of classic fairy tales. There are nine different shows and all the performances are for children aged 4 to 12 years, and for their parents, grandparents and other relatives. *For more information see nederlandsmarionettentheater.nl*

Film

There are several cinemas in Amsterdam, ranging from ultra modern to good old-fashioned. It just depends on where you want to go and of course what movies there are playing. We mention a few. Pathé has four branches in Amsterdam: the **Arena, Munt, City and Tuschinski.** Occasionally Pathé has a special toddler's programme during which the lights don't go out completely and the sound level is minimized. There are also cheap family tickets. The oldest cinema in Amsterdam is **The Movies**. This cinema is worth a visit for the antique interior. Note that most foreign films in the Netherland have subtitles; only when you see 'NL' you know it is Dutch spoken. *See for the movie programme biosagenda.nl or filmladder.nl*

INDEX

PRACTICAL
Apps 8
Emergencies 15
Events and activities 18
History 38
I amsterdam City Card 12
Opening hours 15
Places to stay 15
Public holidays 15
Public transport chip card 11
Tourist Office 11
Transport in the city 12, 30
Transport to the city 9
Websites 8

MUSEUMS
Amsterdam Museum 57
Anne Frank Museum 70
Biblical Museum 64
Dutch Resistance Museum 111
Film Museum EYE 93
Gogh Museum, Van 124
Hermitage Amsterdam 106
Houseboat Museum 66
Jewish Historical Museum for Children 115
National Maritime Museum, The 79
NEMO 80
Rijksmuseum 122
Stedelijk Museum 126
Tassenmuseum Hendrikje 62
Tropenmuseum Junior 113
Werf 't Kromhout, Museum 85

MUST-SEES
Amsterdam Arena 117
Amsterdam Dungeon 58
Artis 108
Begijnhof, The 59
China town 54
Dam Square 53
Flower Market 60
Hollandsche Manege, The 133
Hortus Botanicus 106
Houseboat Museum 66
Madame Tussauds 54
National Monument on Dam Square 53
Noordermarkt 72
Olympic Experience 133
Pampus, Fortress Island 88
Public Library 78
Royal Palace, The 52
Waterlooplein 104
Westertower 69

FUN TO DO
Children's Cooking Café 131
Films 155
Ontdekhoek, The 146
TunFun 105

OUTSIDE
Amstelpark 136
Amsterdamse Bos 134
Animal Island, The 97
Blijburg 87, 151
City Beach North 95
Construction Playground 't Landje 145
Culture Park Westergasfabriek 142
Diemerpark 87
Natureluur, The 145
Noorder playground 73
Strandzuid 151
Tolhuistuin 94
Vliegenbos, The 49
Vondelpark 128
Woeste Westen 144

EATING & DRINKING
Bagels & Beans 104
Bazar Amsterdam 34
Blauwe Theehuis, The 130

loem 88
loem 36 111
lue 61
urgermeester 114
afé Amsterdam 146
alf & Bloom 61
hildren's Cooking Café 131
irma Koek 90
rozz 65
root Melkhuis 130
annekes Boom 78
-kantine 94
ordino 73
agazzino 84
etropolitan Deli 56
onte Pelmo 73
el 62
oorderlicht 96
ain Quotidien, Le 60
ancake Boat, The 85
ancakes Amsterdam 69
izzabakkers, De 111
llek 95
aart van m'n Tante, De 65
illa Zeezicht 71
agamama 64
scuypje 97

HOPPING

liksem & Sterren 88
hildren's bookstore, The 73
lo 4 Kidz 88
amekeeper, The 72
one with the Wind 62
oochem Wooden Toys 128
elden en Boeven 133
genwijs 88
mps and Elfs 131
iggle Store 61
eet in Huis 85
ld dutch Candy Shop, The 71
apabubble 143
Tinkerbell Toys 65

MUSIC, ART & THEATRE

Amsterdam Marionette Theatre, The 155
Bijlmer Park Theatre 155
Dutch Marionette Theatre 155
Hermitage Amsterdam 106
Krakeling, The 154
NDSM Children's Workshop 96
Open Air Theatre Amsterdamse Bos 135
Open Air Theatre Vondelpark 129
Puppet Theatre Koos Kneus 154
Royal Concertgebouw 128
Sound Playground, The 80
Toverknol, The 154
Vrijburcht 86

LET'S GET SPORTIVE

Amsterdam Arena 117
BMX Amsterdam 153
Boat renting 148
Bike riding 151
Noorderparkbad 98